plain sight

plain sight

Steven Seidenberg

ROOF BOOKS
NEW YORK

ISBN: 978-1-931824-86-6
Library of Congress Control Number: 2020931239

Cover photograph by Steven Seidenberg
Author photograph by Carolyn White

 This project is supported, in part, by an award
from the National Endowment for the Arts.

 This book is made possible, in part, by the New
York State Council on the Arts with the support
of Governor Andrew Cuomo and the New York State Legislature.

Roof Books
are published by
Segue Foundation
300 Bowery, New York, NY 10012
seguefoundation.com

Roof Books
are distributed by
Small Press Distribution
1341 Seventh Street
Berkeley, CA. 94710-1403
800-869-7553 or spdbooks.org

contents

plain sight

Shining rancor, the gall of the sky. From this moment forward—
forsaken, delivered. Concede every breach but dissemble the void.
From this moment forward…

φ

To live with the vanity and idleness of a scavenger, stirring the
warm ashes of encampments just departed for that scrap of with-
ered gristle that survives the dying flame. Such is my delictum, if I
have no room for other sins, such the scourge that shackles this
excursus to its foundered frame, a mustering of fragments against
the sovereign gambit of each livid orb, each modal scheme…

To live—to ruin everything. There is comfort in appearance, but in appearing, only torment. Suddenly, it's over. It begins by being over...

φ

The appetite for novelty—the penchant for *derangement*—is empowered by stagnation, by the fear of being fixed within a posture of decline. That other straw men burn before the altar of the idem is not cause enough to join them, to loiter in the comfort of some *transcendental* plan. In time, one takes no succor in the bearing of the witness, in being forced to smut the lens that trains upon the page, so much as in prostration to the pleasures of prostration; the refuge of some harborage between...

Unpledged and indifferent tabernacle, to whom…to what dis-
port…A tale, it was, not of triumph or advancement, but of piti-
less degeneracy, of an *immanent* debouch. It is best to hope for
silence, as a bearing out…

φ

Degeneracy; never an imprecation. In the variance of molder—in
the root that sets its limit—there is progress, there is *aspect*; in the
rending of the cerement, the promise of plain sight…

One remains in thrall to one's own singular dispersion of first causes as long as one is mindful of desire, in thrall to hope as long as one believes that there is something else, that someday something more than what has happened…than what's happened into *happening right now* will cleave the darkness with the taint of new arrivals and so *save the coming day*…

φ

That you are such a one—that there is either you or one or one more you—needs neither proof of expectation nor the testament of signs. I have already spoken, so this paramour of indices reminds the passing gawker—soon a *confidant*—to mind. And so I yield an opening to other applications of this affable mathesis any more or less ingenuous precursor would agree can hardly justify the regress—hardly discharge the digression—without the always subsequent rebuke of manumissions that the voicing of the practicum can't help but guarantee. The same contrived preamble—that the plural is apostrophe—is reared as both remittance and imperious remand, the surest *ad absurdum* one can use to keep the promissory canticle of languor from abandoning its cohort to an endless brink, a final…

If one could disunite the world reflected in this mirror of hypostases from credence—could warrant every idol the completion of its form—then perhaps some *future* sacrifice would serve to cleanse the spoil of its odium, its pretext; would lead me from the figure of a unity assembled to a wholeness *beyond* difference—an exile which is no less *in the fold*...

φ

Necessity without release, a vestige of what never was, the tracery of ruptured seams joins shallows to their sundered depths, as glints upon the verge. Insanable sleep, a tedious poise...

One shouldn't bother saying one needs nothing, or one shouldn't *need* to say it, whether one bothers or no. That I have paid such heed because the order is an affect of its needful contravention is apparent, though that is not precisely my position or concern. What is, I'll tell you now, is not established or forthcoming, for the precedent of something less imagined than proleptic—the genial surrender of diminishing horizons, as a vanishing in aggregate that nears despite the pride of its dispersal, its persistence…

φ

Take my hand; this world forgives. Yours may be quite ruthless and I can't say the correction will exceed the subtle pleasures of this sluggish liberality, or likewise fail to unconceal the other paths—the other *tongues*—by which your mouth discerns the bitter mulct of its own savor, but that seems quite enough to bind you over for a little while, beyond the nearing lookout of this missive affectation, when something else will happen, something still more like a promise— like, but as the image of an absent friend. I can't say that I'd blame you if you took your leave directly, without second glance—or first—to match your own in its discretion; that you'd be less in- clined to sanction such droll marginalia if I cursed the ground you scour on your chafing knees, but that is neither here nor there to one whose vim has managed to begin its final *volte-face*, the craven weal of one whose back has turned…

Neither here nor there inscribes this incidental onset, this indentured spree; the path towards dissolution is made stable by deferment, by offering the transit as a standing in its own right, thus an end achieved. One imagines the predicament of those who failed to see the deluge coming—no time to draw a last breath...

φ

A clearing—a departure—and so the case is closed. The vacancy is tempting—every interval is filled. This, then, is the gist, although the point avers another matter. This is what it comes to—what it *will*, when it comes due. The chief thing is to be seen...

To manifest—to *measure out*—the suffering velleities that inundate each novel excavation of the nous. No flight from isolation is a search for common calumny, either proffered as a warning or a fungible abuse. All tidings, no matter how glad, are made abject by transmission. What we long for is a freedom that's *continuous* with quietus; what we search for is an infinite…a *limitless* abyss…

φ

When I exhaust my powers of description, I'll consider myself disguised. If there were something to be done, if there were some way to *not do it*, I'd return this vain demurral to the portent of surrender. When there's no one left to see you, there's nowhere left…

One must learn to hate one's enemies, but the character to rouse them can't be learned, must be innate…

φ

The secret labor of instinctual decadence, the faculty of looking around every corner—this is what it comes to, what my mastery amounts to, as those disgruntled hierarchs who've gained the right to sacrifice their undiscovered sectaries by having long since sacrificed themselves. Have I said it already? There is no other practice; what is possible for others is not possible for me. What is possible for others…the chief thing is to be seen…

Have I said it already? But when I say already I already grow…have already grown distracted. Already distracted, by having been already made to vanish in diathesis, passing from the servitude of passage to the stasis of this billet in the always in-between. The present is already…the presence of the present is the ready-made already that, contrived as the submission of what has been to what will be, bequeaths the fleeting suppliance of sense to every passing…every passage…

φ

Weary. And distracted. Wearily distracted is the way of all requital. Weary ambuscade portends the triumph of retreating. Impassive brume recoils into substance—into *matter*—where all other formal archetypes advance such change of state as though a symbol and a symptom of our stumble into regress, the *method* of our aimless lurching towards…

All the nothing you see, all the vanishing you phrase—an exultant prostitution to the future…

φ

To find one's place in history one must linger past its limit, one must step aside. To take the role of doyen one must fill the position—the *position*, I say—of prophetic obsolescence; one must make oneself the bulwark of subjection without conquest, without even the *prospect* of advantage, or remise…

These thoughts become too savage to return me to the hope that every similar assignment of opprobrium prefers as an admission, an escape. But perhaps this is enough. But perhaps this is enough. To be regarded. Become at once already once confused. Become distracted. Would like to end. Would like to end. I. A mere moment of clutter initiates our slump into catharsis, if not sacrament. I am learning to have been seen, to have already seen by having been seen. By being seen. Everything else that passes passes over...

φ

Seeing every side precludes the seer from engagement, from the subtle disarray of seeing anything at all. One is first made master of this roiling persistence by submission to the exigence and camouflage of stasis—a *deliverance* from praxis—which is equal to an infinite delay...

To imagine oneself virtuous one must first conceive of virtue as a rhapsody of action, regardless of one's subsequent discernment of effects. That there has been forewarning of the difficulties waiting just beyond the next horizon is no reason to change courses; such pain adduces progress, makes of history the semblance of a reasoned voice. The look back is illumined by the mirror of futurity; no one is a hero to one's debtors, or a scoundrel in one's zeal for second chances…

φ

Of what's been said already, if not by me then by some other, I neither stand as witness nor believe that such crude testament would serve to ground the reverie by which the claim to witness is betokened, thus confessed. Anyone who might conceive this forfeiture of reasonable affect as a means and not a measure…not a measure to be sure of…To be sure it is no matter to the seity whose prescience understands such vacant canon as a *universal* voice. And this, too—this mattering alone—is of no consequence to those who are as useless in the judgment of their rivals as confined within their reservoirs of longings and intents. Only mattering *together* matters…

The marshaling of one's affiliates into an amalgam of instantaneous reflexes requires the proscription of everything else. Exclusion is not merely the effect of common orders of kinship—the feint of consanguinity, both compulsive and by choice—but is equally intrinsic to the nature of discernment; to the indolence of being in a world…

φ

There has to be someone—*anyone*—otherwise nothing. The truth of the matter and the mattering alike is made coherent by the augur of the fragment, the disruption; by the trick of some caesura put upon each ersatz plexus—each perimeter of middles—as a nascent void…

The truth of the eye is its blinking, its lid, of the hand is the fist in its socket, the whimpering snout. The truth of the thumbs and the fingers reflexive, the prints of caresses, the grease of the lips…is the truth of the missive, the tongue in its socket, the truth of the palpating fist in its mouth…

φ

Resignation may appear the pinnacle of temperance, as some discrete surrender to compulsory decay, but only insofar as cause—as *any* sort of purpose—takes the form of its denial, the orderless residuum of vision absent eye. Sovereignty is the price one pays for any *free* reflection; rare is the catastrophe come off *without a hitch*…

Wanting to know what one actually *is*, one sights some wan pulsation of repulsive physiognomy and runs from the assemblage, from the aggregate of seconds that one's indigence dislimns. Then one suddenly perceives it, one discerns the prime of privilege—only those who one has just exalted will surrender, whose nature is to cower from their nature *will proceed*...

φ

Of having said already what I will say, of knowing what I will say will have been said—I think it fair to think this a quotidian epiphany, which anyone who's failed to say it once has done so... has not done so...has *settled on* for fear of its receipt *as though* repeated; for having had the confidence to not say what requires no such confidence in saying to be known. Eschewal of redundancy is the need by which invention finds its valency—its *parlance*. Otherwise nothing...

The hideous opprobrium of the ontic; that one must find a place—
must *take a stand*—within its compass…

φ

Condemned to grieve this deficit of deficits unchallenged, a peon
to the victory of entr'acte over missive—over voice. I face you now
as fabulist and proof of desecration, that while I have propounded
no such posture—no such *transect*—to speak of or have spoken of
already in my time, I'm no more likely to retreat from the remon-
strance than I am to supervene this venal portent with a message,
to begin the *next* divergence with some prolix mise-en-scene…

To claim one holds the truth is first to postulate its access, to wallow in the culvert of perceivable effects. To repudiate the commonplace and still remain a party to the commons of awareness takes a courage more than cognizant or mastered by osmosis, the courage of an innate agitation against sense...

φ

Transcription is the sepulcher of all perturbed specifics—the annealed chiaroscuro of defensible *noesis*—and so does one's detachment from the core of such antipathy impel one's languor forward from its sump of phlegm. One cannot drink from both the source and the mouth of the Nile at once, after all...

After all that has been said is furtively recanted, all that goes unnoticed turns from prospect into trace; after every last awakening to feign the novel pleasures of a new world and a new light of attractions and surmises, and after the abuse of truth—satiety, release...

φ

Dissimulation trumps the vain supremacy of oversight. The brightest star made subject to the seignory of clouds...

Others grope for meaning in a world without consequence, but we wait at the entrance to an infinite compendium, assembled to provision its blockade. It is easy enough to advance future reprisals as the vindication of present importunities, but such affect only satisfies as long as one believes that there is something to be gained by the surrender of the value of all values to the promise of debasement, then dissemblance—*then dissolve...*

φ

And who has thought to whisper such crude persiflage to me? For one whose vim is spent in the procurement of an absolute isolation, what use the dribbled sanction of this callous reportage? What life could reave the tender scourge of such coarse dialectic by defiling the firmament with manufactured wings? This rigid hash of wax and twine, a sputtered benediction gliding over tidal scree—so would pass my portents into histrionic chaffer, so would all celestial mouths have tongues hewn out of rubber, and the tractable grandiloquence of artificial things...

This *anschluss* of beginnings mimes an appetite for suppliance; sur-
render comes again before the afternoon is finished. No conqueror
is sated by a placid abdication; one wants for time to raze the walls
before the gate is opened. Victory; suborn your sick *and weep*...

φ

Fortitude is no more likely to present us with a passage to the truth
than cowardice is to divert us from it. What we long for is not
bounded by the framing of the view so much as by the burden of
our blindness. Thus is the circumference of *occlusion* our
demesne...

As servitors who take so long in making their gruel palatable,
there's no time left to eat before the next task has commenced.
Well, better a ripe pulpit than a fruit tree…

φ

To fight against the steady state commits one to the fallacy of prof-
fering a causatum beyond its stable kind. One occupies one's ampli-
tude as absence, as recusant; one takes one's final chance—*one's last
reprieve*—to step aside…

The field is empty. The games are done. Nothing remains but festival rubbish, all streamers and munition shells. This is where we go, after the fun has ended. This is where we find ourselves, the ditches wide, the mud still warm. It is a good place, and everything is good. To hide in holes already searched—the essence of wisdom…

φ

When the future rises up as clear as a sewer grate through a foot of water and the protean mull of humus sticks to a gash in your shoe like a stare, you have submitted to the privilege of suspecting everyone, of supposing everything an image worth the forfeit of its forfeiture, the truncheon of a prurience made commonweal…

Repetition is not delirious; before the advent of desire the body is bespoke. That the tailor is hardly a craftsman; that one's vision of the future—of the absence *filled*—is no more than a vector in the project of emergence means that such fulfillment only manifests as recapitulation...

φ

The art of denying without making inimical; the art of destroying without *making space*...

No aberration—*as* aberration—is exigent to one's attempts to reach repleted acumen, nor one's parallel concussion into plenary array. A gathering of exiles reveals character only insofar as it is character *in common*; as there is something in the aggregate that forms the very *choosing* of the many who are proffered as exception, or as ward…

φ

Yield to the charm of catastrophe, the climax of a certain convulsion; this is your door to the new way, this is the new way inside the old. Retreat in step with common faith, the topos of a certain break can't hold you back, can't see you through. This is what you *can* do, what your peevish path to dispatch coalesces from the molder; this is where your triumph lies, don't doubt it…

If I were silent I'd hear nothing. No time for inflection. If the pauses are not endless, then they have not really happened. What right have I to stop even a moment? Only the dead have rights, but there are other forms of warrant…

φ

The far-away begins by being within sight. One must glimpse a fixed horizon in the distance for the distance to have meaning, for the promise of the harbinger to differ from mere faith. If some consummate conceit is made to seem a final purview; if the time for second guessing is to come around…

The liberation of beauty from virtue, of death from the dying. Fate is the anticipation of future imprisonments. How else task the vergeless eye—*an ass between two burthens*—against sense…

φ

A room that resembles a dream, surfeited with angles. A stomach of a room, split up floor to transom. A room egressed by trapdoor, tripping into…over…into…This is my abiding stead, this my changeless purview. Here the god of my arousal swallowed by some grubby lintel, there I yield my viscous middle to the ordure of repose. How will I plead, who will receive this turbid spew of lucubrations? Who apply a measure to the missing, or the culled…

The whole structure engendered by blisters; lungs wheeze into raillery, a final transformation. One would like to think the ferment of desire interdicted by forbearance—by the *thrust* of disavowal—but the contrary is true; it's the farrago of sinew—of *putrescence*—that occludes…

φ

Politeness is the most pernicious heresy; the deity addressed with easy gratitude—as a *sovereign* office—is denied its due opprobrium, the guilt for which its *nihilo* effectuates a world…

An unaccountable obliquity when I become surveyor, that most dear of all successions, despite my vain endeavors to keep nothing but the quietus of sacrificial grazing in the languor of my purview, the comfort of my thrall. I have done all that I can, but I have nonetheless been chastened to this venery unchallenged; someday soon the fawn will take the mastiff by the nape. Which is to say I've found my purpose somehow *over*-proved by this ecstatic acquiescence to an incoherent standard, a ravenous degenerate made carrion *to myself*...

φ

But I have no monopoly on stagnation, nor an appanage whose produce is surrendered to some unborn king. I have not been made manic by my manic perseverance, nor is having thus appeared a resignation to regard. Aspire to the vegetal and—duration knows no law. Sometimes we...this intimate plurality I carry as a latent scar...sometimes we fear everything, every *possible* mark. Sometimes I wonder—must I always suffer to avoid beauty? I, too, had dreams before I dreamed this dreamed world from its tacit void, but...

Approbations, denials. The obscene impassivity of inherited vices. One would like to *speak* submission to the dream of form and substance, but no *one* can find a mouth, can force the lips to part…Approbations, denials; but nobody asks *you* anything…

φ

Radical doubt appoints us to the public institution of the soul. The surface of attention stripped of sense and elasticity, we have no greater recourse than replacing our invention of a vigorous transcendence with a lazy null…

I search the ground that promenades before me for the shiny bits, the scrum of scattered moieties beguiled into gleaming. Such sediment may galvanize a negligible squint from those who live in service to more rarefied refinements, but only for the subsequent bequest of such arousal to the wholly exoteric conformations of exchange. Love is an equivocation, equal in all objects of its protean carouse. And one for whom the view is gently whittled from the shadows of a grander scheme will always fail to recognize the commonplace pursuit of this insuperable ransom, the dithering enthrallment of the hidden and the bared. I repeat: All is equal when one loves true. So what that I devote myself to the trifling propinquity of a pebble in the road or the Parnassian grandiloquence of the stars...

φ

Consciousness has three tombs: its body, its world, and its representations...

Some skin burns. A boil fills the hollow. Sometimes everything is lost, sometimes all is ripening to conquer worlds unknown, to scrape discharge out of pustule in a guaranteed subtraction from the scale. I hear whispers in dead languages. I think, *that spot's empty*. I grow brave in my persistence, then—another look. Here the rotting gums restrain a mouth from osculation, there the bead of turned-up glances stimulates a vain remorse. Once on this escarpment laid two lovers whose fecundity resulted in the Black Death. Duration knows no law...

φ

There are readers of the world who are not really readers at all, who find themselves released from such remedial transference by the yearnings of a lofty brood, an eager scorn. And so they ask the secret of all things from last to fore, the meaning of all mysteries and signs that will concern you...

Of everything that will concern you, and all the shreds and clippings of the rest, of pitiful misadventures and star-crossed agonies delayed, I set my shrill compliance without claim to any more or less progressive *ars poetica* and so forgo a maundering reprisal of events in favor of a discipline you're sure to want to replicate, the laborious futility of a character maintained. That there is no advantage to inscribing your conations beyond paying for the common share you've rented *by the mouth*; that you stake your tithe and tribute on a backwardness that locates its reward not in dominion, but *in medias res*—from such idyllic pose you have no reason to reprove what you've been given for a stature, for the privilege of a standing, and so I set my sights on merely keeping you amused. And as I am not likely to make much noise in the world, that voice that you find so much more interior than what was once your own will serve us both as argument in favor of this fealty to appearance, this allegiance to…

φ

Failure binds us to the present, inertia to the future. Above all things, the decadent effectuates a past life *in revolt*…

Successive infiltrations of the revenants whose praxis is the frittering away of present agonies require that I dictate this encomium in something like a mania to ebb from all position—*to bow before the conquered*—surrendering to legionnaires who've yet to leave the womb. It seems an interruption; perhaps there have been many. Perhaps it is enough for an incipient resolve. It seems an interruption; there is nothing else…

φ

A claim you will dismiss, for which I'm not the least bit grateful. I am not grateful, but neither would I make a move to obviate the quip. Is there any form of reason…any quiver into postulate less likely to return us to such stipulated cantor, the hesitant malfeasance of an execrated voice? The question is not idle, but that doesn't mean I'm able to rejoin with any wit. The question is not idle…

Are there any lesser suitors who would not still feign compliance with the presage of so many indistinguishable bludgeons held above them like the pounding weight of atmospheres, a threat not meant to pierce the aching thorax or the noggin but to rend with the slow torment of a turning winch? Is there any other path to reach the terminus I've garnered since the advent of this schism… this schism from all schism from the adventitious clay? Any stalwarts who would not begin to question such glad purpose in whatever they find purpose…who would not start out again if it would help to free their vision from the spectral suppurations of a lineage extended—a preterit for once for all *delayed?* Are there any lesser suitors who appear…

φ

From one stage to the next, the curtain falls. One may find delectation in the antics of the company; may long for the revival of some raucous prank, some cloying song. No matter. There are limits to everything, to every possible devotion. Sometimes one can't help but bow one's head down, but turn away from all observance. Someday every public will have *used up* its applause…

One wants to think the eye set at the apex of a triangle whose base is infinite, to imagine the extension of one's view beyond all boundary or limit, but it is never so, no matter what the phase or balance. There is always an occlusion, an encompassing conspectus; the only view that vitiates the strain of acquiescence is the one that clings unflinching to one's back…

φ

I walk among the fragments of a future only I discern as whole. To redeem what has not happened yet, to parse the cull of meaning from the given, from…

Every victim flushes with the pride of being chosen, singled out for this or that importunate abuse. To judge oneself as something more, to patronize the witness, one must realize that catastrophe is not the gift of silence, but its active simulation of a fate contrived as given, one's ouster from the concourse of all possible results…

φ

There is no alternative, if one has listened well; one must vacate every stratagem contrived as shrewd or prudent and return what one has gained—one has *abducted*—as a Jubilee…return one's plundered haul as though in service to a sacrament, and free each restive vassal baited onto hallowed ground…

Desiccated flesh is indiscernible from dust, but for the chance and unaccountable caprices of the heart. Betrayals that appear to be submissions…

φ

The whole business is mechanical. Pulmotors whistle, entrails twitch with peristalsis. Nosebags filled with pabulum pump easy glee through dull synapses, averting empty stomachs. An irresistible stupor overtakes the convivial faculty—Who repulsed these profligates into such a dull subsidence? What necrotic god lays scales upon these mucid sockets? The transit of the sightline into abscess, into…

Where there is wound without a cicatrix—the hollow space of sight. Regression to departure; I'll be there; I'll say it's me, an overtly paradoxical attempt. One more second. Hold...No consecution binds without a first. Without a first each member is a second—the same second. A spot of blood corrupts the setting sun for our eternity. The gaze has never served anyone, a garrulous distortion. No other sated maw would dare to speak...

φ

A face as heavy as a bag of flour covers you elastically, to think that it's the final...it's the *only* one...The squeak of leather pleats about the neck and chin, the scrape from which the gibbous grin retires into dormancy, is neither heard by those who watch the savage pucker stitch its way from fundament to brainpan nor adduces an inscription by the rectors of design. The carnival of withered lips dreamed victim to benignities whose only other service is to viscerous afflictions; whose last attempt to moisten is at once a sly betrayal of pleasures only fleetingly remembered, if at all. This recondite debasement, this *summa summarum* going dead against mimesis—the first and final messenger endowed to send the message, the inadvertent narrator of what that selfsame narrative obscures...

To write for strangers is impossible; no ego plays familiar to the voice whose conscience limns it. There is no next beginning not beginning in the middle; no image of transcendence, tracing shadows in the desert…

φ

I'm not sure how to warrant such withdrawal—such *divergence*—nor by what agitation of the sea-grass I have come to be the prey of beasts who traipse along the sand. I believe that in some distant life you were more…*so much* more than you are now; but of myself? An old fruit brought in by the tide, its desiccated husk kept lithe with aqueous emollients, thus—degeneracy, that least admired rectitude, proves antiphon to every ruse of suppliance or censure, dreamed or jeered…

To think that it won't work, that if I start again I will have finished finishing…

φ

Character is adduced by nothing so much as obstinacy, even as the singular refusal to refuse. Could one propel one's story as a weary mule, and thereby live it likewise, avoiding all diversionary forage in the service of deferred reward, then one might yet foretell the journey's middle from its start point, and so at last be done with it, for knowing that its terminus will come around…

Absolute power may corrupt absolutely, but short of such unmiti-
gated suasion one's corruption is forever incomplete. Now, of ab-
solute impotence...

φ

Battered and exposed—the political economy of surface. That
somehow something penetrates the unity of affect is neither reason
to accept it nor a method of resistance. The paucity of meaning is
the surfeit of appearance. The industry of absence is...

To all those who have neither felt such umbrage in prevenience nor given themselves over to the sympathetic audit, who know not when—nor even if—their covenant of lineaments betrays a single thing that's felt or seemingly conceded, let them train themselves to succor, to compassionate debasement, let their image of the world seem but another simulacrum of the ditch they will inhabit when their sojourn has completed its collusion with dissemblance, with the feint of declination *in defiance* of decay. To those who have no picture of the cleft their cravings flow through, of the median they plot against such suppliant crusade, let them fit themselves to cower in the sinew they make billet, let them fake their own surrender, by surrendering…

φ

For my part, I thought nothing of fear—I simply grew. Grew past all distinction, beyond boundary or limit; grew to fit the sinecure of nullity which every claim to virtue makes implicit…

To call this a description, this obliquely purled horizon of effronteries aside…to say that there is principle in living past one's limits is not really an avowal I am willing here to sanction, perhaps at some *next* juncture, but no such seems near at hand. It is another matter to promote the contiguity of borders as though something else might fasten roots along the distant shore, the sort of *else* I'd be inclined to seek as much as offer when the moment comes again. As though there were an etiquette to guarantee such promise—or its breaking, a more likely end—but what difference of the kind could thus be fathomed into evidence as portent or presentiment by anyone but its maker, that oft imperiled ego who will countenance its posture of encroachment *and* delay…

φ

Silence is a chance disturbance, an interlude between the growing caterwaul of voices and the votary that hears them, the partisan remainder *that discerns…*

There is a moment in the course of every circumnavigation where one must pick a direction, one must choose a side. The curse of understanding is in knowing that the view won't be the same the next time round…

φ

Does not every deviation trace a circle on its tangent? Every scope adduce a vestige of some long forgotten turn? Surrender is what leads us to the standard, to the *ransom*; conation works the *surface* of the causatum, no more…

You think that I digress, but who stipulated focus? Have I ever in the course of this...this *affinity* of portents seemed to have my purpose advertised with courtesies and blushing glances? Have I scuffed this milky velum in the service of *synopsis*? Or traced a course made up of anything but tangents from all countable...all *fungible* results? And if I could...I could have followed...What difference is there to it in the end. Or the beginning. No subsequent means—no precedent. Good enough. Self-expiation. Expiate. *Enough...*

φ

There are those readers, I am given to understand, who feel themselves abandoned if they can't attach a tow line to the scudding prow of narrative excisions vainly roiling this storied bilge; who'd rather gulp down waste wash with the ardor of a glutton than be forced to sip and savor the most rarefied of wines. And though I do not count myself as either sort of vintner—who would feign decant the sewers or distill some cherished yield—there is something in my purpose that repulses, that dismembers; something that inherits without lineage...

History consists in making of resemblance an ontology, a cull for which the practice of divulgence seems anterior, as a sequence of appearances intractably compelled. One finds a pleasant moment in assuming the disinterested demeanor of reflection and the world becomes an index of ecstatic reenactments, a pleasant abdication to the refuge of remembrance, as a hunter's blind…

φ

Formerly, each end held the promise of a new beginning. Now, the sky has opened, the erosion of the future is integral and—this blighted mound is all that's left, a Calvary surveyed…

Why should *you* complain when nothing but such divagation has made overtures to fitness, has foretokened your retreat across this ruptured, static rime? If *I* can't find a reason to remit *ab ovo* every lame caprice that countermands this paltry service—this impertinent travail of anabasis and delay—then why assume such fury at my spurning of the question, the question you have yet to have the fortitude to speak? Why should I await your bashful scorn to find expression when, to turn a phrase, I might as well head off your ragged legions at the pass...

φ

The philosopher rejects conviction, not for fear of falsity, but because it is extravagant; because, like all intemperance, it cannot be maintained...

Eschaton or atrophy—if one insists on sheltering behind some *meaning* stasis, why not choose the stasis of depravity, of corruption; of the final...the *inexorable* negation of the same...

φ

I have endeavored, so you see, not only to indite my peevish gaze into existence, but also to avow the world that fashions its forbearance at the threshold of that barren span. You must in turn have patience, although precisely for what purpose—and to what peculiar end—I'm not ready yet to say. You must have patience *with yourself,* and thereby nothing that has moved me will seem trifling in its nature, or tedious to the pretense of my project—or its vagrant aim...

In order to be generous, one must have something to give. One must grow hair before one can have lice…

φ

Go ahead, laugh with me or at me, skip a page or two and start again with more companionable jargon; it is your right to blot the pages with tears or linger long and without focus on the cover or the binding, only—keep your temper. Of long faces there are two sorts; that of grief's drudge and that of the imposter. Only you know which is yours…

A destiny destroyed is a destiny fulfilled. The freedom from all longing, from the *connate* will…

φ

To realize the necessity of failure is to embrace a private madness, the enigma of an infinite singularity; to arrogate the paradox of limit without border, of border without bound. That I thought the immemorial passivity of turning back an invitation to the primacy of indigence was my attempt…my *futile* attempt to counter madness with madness, with the frenzy of reaction; to controvert accession to the stasis of catastrophe with a catastrophic ferment, and thus replace the itch with a remediable scale…

Disabused of both illusion and the lack of illusion—the obligation to be nothing ever again. What more could you ask for? Don't answer. What more could you want? What less…

φ

My mood clots quickly; I have seen the death of my children from a distance, as a figure in a crowd awaiting the suicide's leap. Of other indiscretions…well, what is there to say. We all have fore-bears. Even tumors can lay claim to genealogy, though what that has to do with it…I will neither say what that has to do with it nor admit that that has anything to do with it. Let this empty exegesis both suffice us as a model—a fundamental *principle*—of explication, if you will, and present the measured foreground…the *frontispiece* of our compelled repletion in the giving of the given, the tautology of the found…

What distinguishes my life from the lives of others is not so much the *fact* of my abjection as its fatality. I'm surely not the first to take my impulses for quiddities, nor is there any reason to believe such feats of reasoning would have otherwise gone missing from the catalog of idioms had I but once forgotten to remember their elision…

φ

This is my minimum; who has granted me another? The naming of a surface is already an assertion of its limits—of its *measure*; the distinction of its status as some next-to to which I have been apportioned the most commonplace of adits, of expedient defer-rals—that which is presented to those dullards who have made their way from one evaluation of the value of all values to another, then another still. It's not so much to mention for a first course, not so little either, but…

The welts on a cadaver hold more promise of arousal than any fur-
ther cant of my incendiary idols, but for all the fatal prospects I've
indifferently compelled into this palace of departures, I will not
risk the dudgeon of returning to the prime. Fatal for whom, you
ask—So be it. I ply you with benevolence, with the pledge of
winsome pleasures, and what do you give me? Riddles. What am
I to do with riddles...

φ

The camouflage of stimulus, the patience to give voice to an
illimitable stillness. Suddenly, everything must appear; even absence
seems ephemeral, a mere anticipation—of the mere...

They climb the peaks and swim the seas in search of El Dorado, disabused of pity and consenting saturnalia by their ditch into the baffle of pecuniary slog. We crawl and they step over us; we think their shadows vultures. Will they notice that our decadence has started to unfurl our stench, our next compelled progression towards the blunder of composure? That our last chance is upon us? That we've rolled back on our heels? So let them come; we have no better care than that our flesh falls off tomorrow, as though the master scavenger prefers a vintage gruel. Let them mouth the supple bits that decompose with the best savor, that slip past glugging gullet while the tongue lolls to and fro. The suppliant sees last the ventured promontory bulged against the pleasures of engorgement, the ransom and release of every vulture felled...

φ

To think that I have done so much to pace my derogations, to keep myself from spitting in the face of my *next* kin. And this despite my confidence that not a one is willing to avow their useless fealty, to play consort to this tableau of putrescence...

The problem is discernment. There is nothing wrong with your nerves. If I said it were my purpose to invert every impertinence from what had once appeared its near infinity of prospects—from all prospects of allegiance, either extent or ideal—then everyone would settle on their way without a tactic, and I could have it out… *have out with it*, that is, while trammeled in this curdled pause. Discernment: that one should not mistake the brash demeanor of the hedonist—the prodigal impenitent awaiting an untold reward—for the portentous imprimatur of a dull wit…

φ

The invention of a second does not help to free the speaker from the voicing of that inadvertent cynosure of norms, whose only fault is having always spoken up too soon and never at the moment that would do the most to service the regard of that who speaks it—of its speaker somehow undisclosed by being *spoken to*. If you've failed to ask the question I've ascribed to your imprudence—a median whose level is not more or less authentic for the lack of any reference to its placement in the world—you only have yourself to blame, and that with very little in the way of such droll clearance from this cordon of inconsonant…what postures as this muster of *incongruous* refrains…

If there are limits to my compassion for the broken-hearted, it's not for having been denied the ache of such immurement, but for realizing my captivity has never been complete. The maundering of every gurgled absence into fragment is enough to cordon off this nervous courtesan from penance, to bungle all attempts to keep my flaccid heart strings taut...

φ

That there is little to distinguish this commitment to the plague of understanding from its curry with the common thrall is not my concern; I bring it up to stave off the next paragon of diatribes and droll prognostications that has surely just begun to intimate a different course, that one might take one's pleasure in another vain perusal of the novel and the fated, of the given and the found. Again, not my concern. I do what I can to help the stranger when the circumstance avails. If that's not enough, well, take your ticket, mind the queue, and you might get the chance to knock some sense into me yet. I'll be the one...

The content of one's dreams has no bearing on one's talent for dreaming. An idiot's wrathful reverie is no less difficult to limn— nor wearisome to *recount*—than that of some more philosophic malice, a proof by demonstration of the vassalage of forms to their concrescence. In this, if this alone, every substance that is placed *behind* appearance is made equal and indifferent, made a subject to its predicates; in this, if this at last, we are sublimely disabused…

φ

The grotesque trivialities of the autonomic, the dreamless squalor of the everyday; the peddle-pump of latency assigned its vim and surfeit, its forced carouse. A layer of filth lies between us, but I can still make out your margins. I can tell that you're still with me by the slough you've left behind…

One identifies as speaker when one struggles to keep quiet, as cheat when one recalls the idle promises of comrades just as ready to betray a trust as burden its possessor with the prospect of dependence, the whisper of that priestcraft that makes all the world a stage. And if the silence is a comfort—if the noise is *disconcerting*—is the ailment in the system that has limned its peace in fine or in the respite that has gifted us the certainty of meaning *less*, of passing from conviction into cynosure, *then screed…*

φ

To conceive of one's own personhood—one's *consciousness*—as agent, one must open up a socket set beside the thinking of it; one must strike up an acquaintance with one's floundering substantive as though it were intrinsic—as though, that is, there were no *in* but what the *out* excludes…

The harlequin's coiffure, contused with bootblack and macadam, will maintain its ludic loft against all passionate caress. Go ahead and spit your worst into that tumid rookery, stomp the muscular glimmer of the bloated cheeks, the wilted crest; let the molars ground to dust secure the jowls against the rotting loam, the spastic mince, that will not budge but for the fateful slingshot of the fist in gut, the knife thrust into rigid hump and ploughed through slackened viscera; that will not shy from reverence, from gratitude for sour mash, nor trim a suit to suit a merely stipulated lenity, so pave another listless road with molting gore and bad intents. That lastly will not importune the Gordian knot of valor for a cherished vow, condemned to bliss...

φ

Nothing but discernment—the subjunctive of the beautiful—results from our discretions, from our choosing not to indicate our choosing not to choose. One must destroy all bridges, clear the view of all horizons; one must trill without the prospect of applause to claim this opiate estrangement. And frolic in accretions of dissemblance more complaisant than the sigh between two eschatons, the lull that gleans the promised *from the real*...

The prophet proven soothsayer is reviled, then dispatched. Unheeded, such injunctions appear juvenile challenges, but once they read as certain they seem purposed to humiliate, to spread the plague of virtue by prognosis—then despite…

φ

This voluptuary schema is a seignory of swindles, a perimeter of flesh absent all reference to a middle. One need not garner predicates to start the long descent that will occasion one's dismissal of the self-same, of the…I, for instance, have just begun to realize I've been taken, I've been chiseled; have only this first inkling of the speed with which the cheater's stake withdraws from any hand dealt from a new deck. The turning of all chance upon its head denotes a proper bluff…

The truth of the catastrophe—its incidental *aftermath*—draws us out of credence by despoiling our deities with the succor of elision; by cleaving *consummation* from the roster of celestial gifts. It is easy enough to move towards one's conclusion when it cowers in the distance, but to wallow in its immanence…

φ

A petulant homunculus agitates within me. I know its pleasures well, but my indifference makes it disregard all continence for anger, for the scorn that always persons my transactions and amendments, no matter who they spurn or what they claim. One can only imagine its frustrations, a figurehead whose piddling prerogative goes unheeded by the subject on whose will its next satiety depends. Yes, one can only imagine it. And with each tantrum it grows smaller, and its influence declines…

Every birth may well be understood a resurrection, but we can't know of what. Assuredly not character, which can only be adduced by breaking free of all reprisal, by returning every pustule of conation *to the soot*...

φ

I *arrived* here a malingerer; it's all the same to me *where* I am bored...

If only there were some way to avoid the deprivation that accompanies this colloquy, to countermand all commerce with the dissidents who've come to share my fate. If only I could find the means to set my fears beside me, so to stand against...And I suppose I have. The pain of your absence is no longer with me. The pain of your *witness* still accompanies my back...

φ

One is only vigilant in unfamiliar places. Every new arrangement of the furniture holds dangers one can't properly anticipate from an otherwise accustomed stand. Look there—the eaves are bearing down upon the gutters. Turn round—the walls are crouching for the ambush, then the kill. What happened to the doorways? They were eaten by the moldings. Who's stolen all the windows? Perhaps they took their leave...And who could blame them; who would question such an instinct when the beasts that bend the floorboards are so close to an alightment, the wolves that press the tapestries are nearing an escape. So would I decamp if I were not as fully certain that my scent would guide the venery I'm fleeing to my landing, which would by dint of circumstance—the moira of rebellion—be my last. So would I vacate this world if I could only be assured that there would be no I to quit the next world, and the next...

Why can't the sun rise in the West? What else has been discovered? Someone's about to enter. One must destroy all bridges…

φ

Let us understand that our demand for understanding—the hocus-pocus commonweal of shared, hermetic worlds—is all that makes our milieu of discrete participations a necessity—an *existence*—without which nothing less than *dissolution* would prevail. Thus—one's life with others, the catastrophe delayed…

One cannot differentiate one's power over body from one's appetite for conquest, for subordinate abstraction or correlative control, which is only to affirm that the distinction between mind and its corporeal phronesis is constitutive, is the project of *assemblage*— our passage and resistance to the ravaged ground…

φ

To be seen while still unseeing circumvents the languid seizure of the sighted, the torpid sum and aggregate of all that is surveyed. It is too much, it is *too painful*; a surplusage of predicates glut over every stanchion and contrived to fit the warrant of fixed vistas by the slapping palms, the lashing seams; to simulate the shimmer of a landscape in memoriam, and thus construct a cenotaph *all eyes*…

Perhaps I could be prompted to accept such disposition; I'll entertain the prospect of the prospect, nothing more. I'm certain that the tone of my construal means I've pondered it—that I'm pleased with my attempts to meet the challenge, the *ordeal*—and so that the solution has been far less true than tried. Than tried, I say, I've tried it—to be overlord and master, to contrive myself an oculus fixed limpidly beside the spectral union of the luxus, so to cast off from attachment neither shriven nor descried but simply seeing, simply seeing, as a glutton whose esophagus is castigated open, a *camera obscura* made to swallow up an image of the only ever outside, of the…

φ

But this is not my quandary; my problem is a different kind. For when I yield to pabulum—as that is what's on offer—I do not give *myself* but steel the anguish of my ilk against all further importunity, making sure that what returns to me is but another daze of yearning taunts and vengeful parries; that my mastery of mannerist opprobrium decays into the slobber of conation, training every sense to dullness, turning every glance aside…

And when I watch the multitude strut zealously about me, unsated by my diet of insipid rime; when I seek a finer pleasure at the tables of abundance, consuming every blighted pill and poultice I descry, I find I am not only made immobile by the excess, but that bolted to the spot I nearly rupture at the seams. Or grasping just as help-lessly the lathered tide that whelms me, stretching orbits over wings that bend to parry every probe, I am stricken by the loss of even those I haven't met yet, tormented by nostalgia for each next unwelcome stare. Yes, they turn upon me, working solely from the inside, gnawing playfully through viscera that gather from the spume. This cosmos is a tumor I am tenderly neglecting, a leach stuck to the palette, an abscess on the brain…

φ

A retinue of revenants that no locked door excludes. Our holy prostitution—an ineffable orgy—is neither shriven by restraint nor made a captive to resolve. Complaint is useless—there are no next caresses for malevolent hands. Still, one hopes for something, that one's phlegm won't taste as sweet after exposure to the wind. Made *al dente*, as it were, by desiccation…

Masters servant to their mastery. A platitude that doesn't rate the trouble of repeating, but…it seems it hasn't stopped me, and…a maxim far too obvious to mention, but…

φ

Sometimes waiting is preferred. Preferred to doing. Sometimes waiting is the only preferable doing. And what's the good of such admission to the one who entertains it? What difference if one *knows* the truth or struggles to impugn it; one is condemned to *live* it, either way…

When every incidental glance presumes innate antipathy, shifting in an instant into affable assault; when every barbed collation of malignities attempts to leap the rift between impertinent palaver and the loving blush—the fond affront—then what is one to do but turn away, but turn away, *but turn away*...

φ

It seems you've made your point; perhaps I've made it for you. No matter. None of us is one voice. First the lamp of youth bears witness, then the flame spreads wide, but not as brightly. The stranger standing next to you thinks *you're so old*. So be it. As long as you believe the melting snow still bears a tincture of the passage that you wearied from its loft when it first fell...

No detail is more scrupulously rendered from a vantage set above it; the strain of apprehension is not lessened by coherence or some corollary overture to acumen or postulate—by the figure of an infinite *fenced in*...

φ

If the coming of catastrophe were equal to its advent—thus accession to recurrence the means and not the measure of the will to move aside—then one would know precisely when one's time was at its limit—the buttress of its *end point*—and disappear forthwith...

It may seem that my answer has not specified a question, that I've somehow obviated every possible response. It's true that I know nothing of…have no *image* of transcendence—that all my ready ships have long since foundered into port—but I've conceived this puzzle for the pleasure of the solving, not the promise of solution, thus the bungling abortion of the telling of the tale. And though I'm sure my system pales in straight ahead comparison to that devised by circumstance, I do not take that difference for a proof of what it's lacking, but—an unremitting optimist and consonant contrarian—a license to take umbrage and…

φ

And when do I find time for such exacting avocation? When I'm not writing the book I'm not writing now, of course. And where do I find it? Right here, within this garret of meridians—*of course*. One is as likely to find comfort in the middle of the Atlantic ocean as in the bleary chambers of some editorial office…

It is a common enough mistake, though often without consequence. One settles on the practice of dismissing the interminable spate of sensibility in the hopes that by so doing one's own decrepit spreading out from middle to meridian will lay fallow—will find *solace*—perhaps the only point of such repose that ever crosses from the phantom of arousal to the sponge that sops the sky. Mistake, that is, for any who would turn from the anxiety of distance would be deprived the rapture of transcending the next lookout, of uncovering the canker just beneath the burnished peel. Which is *only* to claim that the practice *does* have consequence, and that it is a consequence inconsequential to the masquerade its terminus amounts to—that its genesis *presumes*—and *not* that such mistake is a pursuit of understanding and not judgment, as it seems. The practice has a consequence, presumes some form of gain; the gain is what compels us, but only in the short view…

φ

To live one's fate one must deny the futility of all attempts to thwart it, accepting that recusancy has played a central role in the construction of the world one leaves behind…

If every empty space bespeaks the certainty of filling, whether with some meager billet or some autocratic range, then the quantum of fulfillment rests in certain aggregation, the extension of one's corpus through the semblance of the void. The standing of such want is unrelated to assurance, the ascription of our sovereignty with reference to attempts; just as exploit is not measured by some mere potentiality, the *failure* to achieve only refers *once it's complete*...

φ

One's judgment of the character of judgment has no bearing on the way the faculty thereby adjudged is understood as that—as a *thing judged*; the predilection for some single constitutional proclivity over others has nothing to do with the nature of *proclivities*, nor is there any reason to subject the one thereby exposed to the freeze and scald annealments that the narrator compels...

Isn't it enough that a particular procedure will attain its fitting terminus with some considerable dexterity to have *that* standard justify its choice from all the rest? That of the many paths towards the same end there may be one or two which under similar conditions will be quickest to relieve the weary traveler from forbearance, to petition an escape from the clear boundaries of want? And yea, all this polemic, when not only do I fail to buy this slipshod simulation but have no intent to sell it, thus to gain its loss in kind...

φ

Conscience is the only idol suitable for fashioning, for *carving out*. One who is wise as well as honest satisfies the need to cobble emprise from recalcitrance by playing the impenitent redactor as a pious trope...

Everyone has always just lost sight of the reflection—the parallax encompasses both impulse and effect. Having finally borne witness to the absence of a witness, the catastrophe is no longer merely imminent, it is fixed in its arrival, it is *evidently past*…

φ

I don't know, I say again—though that I've said it yet remains un-certain. I may not be the easiest of raconteurs, but that is not your lot to choose, any more than it's my burden. If only I could lower the pennant of this defensive disregard and lure my lame surveyors to the leap across…I can't face finishing the gest. Or I have no notion *how* to finish it, and there are some thoughts that, unfinished, are most perfectly adept…

Setting aside my innate perversity, my pleasure in defiance of assured recrimination, my imperious elation and the ease with which I use it to discover and dispose of my accusers…what else is there. I will not give what started as abhorrence the status of conclusive proof. This is *not* an act of bracketing, of tracing the horizon; no indolent accession to some preternatural archetype of the face…

φ

Given my near infinite directory of deficiencies, I'm also many other things, things that might well go unnoticed were I not possessed of predicates that bind my fevered contours to a home-stead in this sullen prank. My proof of the first point—that I am not only a decadent, but also its opposite, the *ne plus ultra* of all stoical detachments—is found in my many good works. Go figure. I'm not one to proffer faith as expiation of the damned. More later. Maybe. And of the second? I suppose *this* is the place for my reduction to the simple—my excision of these foundered balks and aspirant rebukes—in order to make *sense* of all that's left. Indeed, this trivial assertion of intent is all I've got; the mere suggestion of the practice abrogates the need to carry out…

Perspective is not vetted by resemblance, nor is the world we part-
ner made a servant to the prospect of its witness—its incipient
surrender to regard. All of which exempts a lesser spirit from
uncertainty, concerned with little more than steady commerce of
the herd with heaven's stockyard…

φ

And if it's not enough—if this *whisper* of an argument can't satisfy
your craving for a sharper line, a finer cusp—then perhaps you
ought to take a good long look at what's at issue, take the chance to
reconsider your position in this venture, that you might find a way
to take my point. Or come to it. Perhaps the sky will open and—
everything's different. Everything's clear. Which is to say…

How easy it is to give the impression of being outside meaning—
beyond the *possibility* of coherence—despite every attraction and
repugnance that accosts the humble speaker as a privy source of
pride. How much we reveal of our desire to conclude our lives in
our lust for decision, for a *terminal* satiety; how much of what we
stipulate as characterization is a corollary reflex, an adjunct to our
agitation forward...

φ

The end of the age is the burden we carry, the burden of clearing
the stars from the sky with our breath...

Should one ascertain the dereliction of depleted space, the scintillating lie of shear discernment, or seize upon the urge to take a closer look, but from a farther distance, then I suppose I'd like to think there'd be some further condensation…some *abridgement* of the suffering, of its adventitious raiment; that somehow one might sing above the canticle of coming wounds, the incidental caterwaul of rot. And I *would* think it, think it through, if the thinking could avoid the same propitious disaffection, but the mere feint of transcendence—of escape *before* immurement— would require something less than an adherence to the principles by which such flight is generally conjectured and effected, and that sort of a thinker is precisely what I'm *not*…

φ

What I *am*—now that's *another* query, if you'll grant me the embarrassed grace. And I expect you will; that's precisely the sort of interlocutor you are. The charitable sort. Still, having already… having always just already required of my host an interminable series of indulgences, I feel comfortable in positing this one as the last—for being the most open to expansion over everything, for finally proclaiming what I've held to from the start, the plenary beneficence that forms as comprehension, that makes *purpose* out of merely giving voice…

What I am; why not just get on with it, and shut the door for good. Well, where would be the fun in that. An ingenuous apologue, if ever there was. If I could but accomplish the position with such careless ease, then perhaps I wouldn't; perhaps I'd deftly sacrifice alacrity for sport. Is there not a greater pleasure…a more palpable *achievement* in plucking out the dead hairs of a horse's tail with one's teeth than in doing just the same with steady hands and steel-pinned tweezers? Where's the thrill in conquering the crowd by force of argument? The pleasure of an armistice—a treaty of surrender— *without threat…*

φ

No affect of ascendancy, no claim to prepossession. This fable will not yield up its prerogative to an inventory of its narrator's traits— and that, again, not for some daring ruse of deference, but for knowing that such pose must first mistake the happy circumstance of prescience for the parasitic fealty of a selfdom fit to size. One must progress, who finds a path; one must tramp stalwart into…

But I have no such luck, nor fit that augur of an end. It has only just occurred to me that I am no one, I am nothing. Or *to say* that I am nothing, to declare that it's occurred to me I'm nothing. Which I have accomplished. Deferring all discussion of the placement of such longing in some erstwhile demurral, it constitutes a change in course that has resulted in many things, not the least being the revelation that it did, at one point or another, occur to me that I was what I would be, which is—not to belabor the point—nothing more than nothing less, than nothing…

φ

I suppose it's true I have some sort of *dis*position on my side, or in my favor—the side of rancor and regret, in short, of existence. It requires only waiting—the merest practice of forbearance—for me to enter in on this most delicate of debasements, that without a seeming change of face or waver of direction I am able to keep at all times one foot in the dying world and one foot beyond dying— in the quinta of the absent, of the dead. It's neither my fault nor my desire; my meager affectation of a middle—of a *rented* pith— finds freedom only there. That I must pay for this privilege with the rest of my life is not unreasonable. I would pay more; I feel certain that *I will*…

Go ahead and look down from a second story window, or from some terraced esplanade hung up a mile high—the scavengers hold court for all who would attempt to soothe them, and no matter your detachment from the plain of their prostration, they will either keep your pity hot or strip your conscience clean. Whatever the compulsion carried forward by such countenance, if you have the rank to see it—to compel it into frame—you've sidled one step closer to your own fateful debasement, a progress surely quickened by the failure to consider the declension as it *starts*. There is no better view, no single seed to sow or harvest; you may ply your trade of clemency or spite to your own ends; go ahead, step to the curb, and soon you will be with them, look down now, as you're seething—you have long since lost what chance you had to die in truth by being born to…born into…being born to be born into…

φ

One clings to trivialities—to one's trifling indiscretions—not to abjure the consequential, but to confront it. Nothing so deflating as the pettiness of absence—of what one *had* presumed would prove the *majesty* of the void…

Everything must appear, this is the rule. That my confession scans as counter to the crime that it confesses—that it may seem *contradictory* to train this wighted hump of vain inducements to a voice that seeks to escort its transhumant host into a boundless null—is a defect that can't vindicate the vigor of denial, or ostensible repair. That I have not run riot over such appeals is miraculous; that I will soon return to the defense of my position—the position of no one, I remind you, of a bubble in the sea—need neither be confirmed nor castigated by reproof. Everything must appear...

φ

Fill me up with boredom—the boredom of emptiness—I am at home. Soon our exile from truth will seem our exile from illusion...

It is painful to realize that surfaces corrode, that moist beds molder while one sleeps, that one has nothing, nothing and no one, remembers no one—that no one remembers anything or anyone beyond the circumscription of one's cobbled reach. But don't fret; no need to search the world over for one brief moment of deliverance from the rule of loss. Don't fret; such anguish will not expiate one's servitude to decadence—which is *its own* reward…

φ

Sometimes I feel as if I have exceeded this dominion of exigency, this gapeless viscera of hollows, but the means by which that cataract of semblances awakes the gulping pharynx from the customary din of creeds endorsed but hardly followed is not what one who otherwise takes passage through each day as some presentiment of outcomes would have thought it—a progression or decline of any *measured* sort at all…

Listen for the cunning clone of seity in reference; no singular discerned as such is able to exceed its brink, its liminal paresis for a laminated essence. Feel the lurching portent pin your inert ells like insect wings upon the ashen pulp of rancid sward and mottled canvas, bracketing the calculus of entropy in onion skin, the suppliance of every hull invented as a dermis. Understand that everything's different, that the door is always open for the exile from betterment, the apathetic seer staring languidly across the bane of barriers erected by the blind...

φ

There are two states of existence—the diseased and the ecstatic—and one is never free of either, one is always stuck between...

You need not feel you need not feel the pain of every victim as the sin of your own comfort; you too have lives to tolerate, a retinue of revenants to countermand—to *down*. But the truth is that your next attempt to sacrifice the privilege of indifference to the concordat of squalor is nothing—*means nothing*; that no pain is severe enough to remedy the trespass or remit the peal of plaudits that accompanies your funerary traipse across the vale. You may not sense the burlesque periphrasis of your agonies, the merciless redundancy in every prick and twinge; you may not know that all you do to compensate the suffering of others—the most rigorous avowal of retractions and amendments—is both deftless and abortive, but *it is*…

φ

I would have given you everything—*everything*—and walked away like a beggar. I would have been happy to give everything to you… to only you…had you remained…had you pushed through…

If *being* is equivocal—without discrete advantage; if there is nothing to commend the *situation* of the exile to the marshaled imprecations of the stars…If longing is a game of gates made level by the promise of amusements still to happen, and so despite this revel in the torpor of subjunctive rant, this bracket of acquaintance lathered into blinding thrall…If no one thinks of nothing, if— your present liege excepted—there is reason to redeem the profanation of your humbled squint, your desecrated scale, then…Perhaps it is a benefice *to have been*, and…

φ

Blind orb, muted heart. A shroud of frost conceals the conclave murdered in the summer. Rot and scald. Return to plot, to probe with ludic antigens and deliquescent fingers. One day—redemption from all conquest, though the spoil is dissembled. This is—a sanctuary from the squall, a door left open…

Images of loss dissolve replete sanctifications. One feels one can
do anything; the sovereignty of lonely hours. A sentient thrust, a
wind blows through—the turgid chaparral divides to let the carriage
pass. Who's approaching? Not you. You're already here, you've
stood your ground, unlike the rest. One feels one can do anything…

φ

I wait for this impenitent contumely to be taken for confession, to
be swallowed whole. I wait to follow you unseen into the addled
frenzy of this pulsing breach, this throng of wounds. There are
moments when I find myself almost returned to patience, to
feasibility, against all odds—and then it's over, it's done. If there
were something of the static in the order of succession I might
endeavor to describe it, thus…

A limpid cage of tedium, this ravaged girth, this wont of rule. Nothing is excluded but—transition, which is all that means. One must endure as *something*—as the absence of *no* thing—in order to dispense the dream of oneness from alterity. Half waking, half in sleep, the world is always filled with cankered pokes and grubby stanchions. Every drunken hiccup seems a masterpiece of plastic art, a scudding retrogression from dyspepsia to gnosis. What have you to do? The doctors come—they go away more often. The doctors say your nerves are fine—but you make *them* nervous. A poultice, then a groping palm…which you am I? Who tells the world *the difference*…

φ

And thus, there is no end to it—so that the end appears the point of infinite persistence, the failure of continuing what cannot yet be finished, what only expands further the further one moves through it, requiring a fidelity to the rigors of digression for the clearest view. In brief, I shall tell nothing about you, nothing at all, not because we have deceived one another, but for knowing that no harm could ever come from such a telling, that only by returning to your absence—the redundancy of returning to your absence—could one hope to discern anything beyond its mean distortion, unbound from the compulsive sleight of stepping off, or coming down…

Again the walls devise escape; this is perhaps their last chance to achieve a common ending, to *prefer* collapse. It's tiresome, only meeting at the crossroads. One would like to touch the lips, to feel the hair stand on the nape. One would like to grieve again, to be no more mistaken for the leavings of a sudden swell, a world caved in…

φ

Attempt to withstand stimuli, affect phlegmatic steel where you would otherwise feign malice. Attempt to stand stock still, to be encompassed by the meek surround of teary glances. Do as you will, give in beneath the clabbered veil of visions undecided by some numen or its fallen brood, a tidal wash of motives neither spoken nor elided, but…It's all I am, my only drive—a foundered barge induced to rolling over by the promise of a next *put in*, a nearer sail. I take no other tonic and—surrounded by insentience—am lured to sip the gall of ataraxia by my own accord. It is only among the silent that the world decays, that decay is made a virtue; only the silent speak escape from our sodality, the final manumission from our common goal…

To say I've wrenched this recto from a farrowing oblivion is to make more of inscription than of prudence or of wisdom, to proffer the ascendancy of archive over vision—the incidental threshold of this waxing cull. If I can rest content with such an empire of inconsequence, it's only for not knowing what the bastion of its outside—its incipient *remainder*—would include…

φ

We all adhere to principles—a principle we all admit. For some, this fitful rubric schemes the next page as an ink wash, for others there are reasons to stay in the queue, submit to what has come before, and importune the sanction of the next in line, to postulate the nearness of a first. For my part, I'm impartial. Take directive where you can, *it's all you'll get…*

I have not found a motive or a warrant to adhere to, nor posed a guiding axiom to synchronize my lusts. Which is only to suggest that my first premise is made portent in precisely this elision, my endless abdication of all sense of proper place to others sometimes near, sometimes at distance, but who nonetheless will only see my back. Who I *will not* see, which amounts to the same difference, the same profit in the wherefore, the same comfort in the proof. And this, I'm loath to offer, not for fear or ease of action, neither action nor amazement turns my vacancy to trance; it is all importunity, the dissonance and umbrage of this feckless troth…

φ

The stillness of the dead is what we signal by transcendence. Dip your finger twice into the Elbe—good enough. The river is equivocal, you've got no clearer standard, but—*it's you who've changed…*

Reflection is the benefice that animates contumely. One is never safe from ghosts convulsed to sullen contemplation. Our only recourse: apology. Avoid mirrors. When the time comes, take your lumps. There's nothing else to do—no way to get used to it. When the time comes, apologize. Let them have their fun. Of appearances it's best to remain indifferent…

φ

I do not weep for what I've lost, but for all that I *will* lose when I have finally lost everything; for realizing that someday I'll lose everything, that everything will come to seem the cover of a lack. It's not some vain nostalgia, but a longing for a time already given up to silence, the deferred dissatisfaction of a rendered host. As though every last feeling were imposed by some third party, some dead member…Every until this one, which is mine *alone*…

Portraiture invigorates the misanthrope in everyone—the loathing that foments to weary virtue from conation. One must appear not merely as another but as an *inhuman* other, a passport to embodiment that is *only* intended, that has never really happened…And who are you, my friend, that you possess such an indifferent grin? A murderer and a thief—you have slaughtered an ox and stolen its face. They say—*It's a fine likeness. You've never looked better.* And so the very fact—the *seeing clear*—of your appearance is the truth of your abjection…

φ

One must overcome pity sometime, somehow. I propose *becoming pitiful.* Commiseration with one's subordinates is easily achieved, but with one's overseers? A ready salve, a proof of strength, and so the visionary puzzle of this spotlight daze—If my elation is the height of excess, why isn't my despondency the extreme of moderation…

The slashed world traced and traced again into the viscous ether of the oculus. No soul, no backroom window trains the orifice to votive scan, the cunning whims of maquillage to pillory or sacrifice. Who trusts image ransoms nature. Betrayed by an ideal decay, the final hostage...

φ

Watch me give my breath away then siphon off the spoil, the moldered meat grow nearly moist for near a week with the injection of an inert jus. See my aspect vanish in the torpor of a polished cheek, my convalescent bodice—stitched of eiderdown and sinew—slowly melt into this sickbed of a curdled white, a parchment blank, swallowed like a screw in the wall...

The perfect painting veiled by sloughing pellicles of varnish; the repulsive patina of poverty, a tar-soaked insurrection—derogated metaphors by which I mean to suffer through the luxury of being always sighted by the dotards of a Roman weal, a priestly scorn. Not that one needs metaphors to satisfy such judgment, but…No. One *needs* metaphors. Metaphors are all that stand between a teeming scullery and a harvest of tares…

φ

The same decadence that ensures so many of our pleasures are impossible to realize mollifies us with the relative felicity of avoided pain, of a gash benumbed. The conciliations of abeyance—the refinements of *expectancy*—pose enough of an allusion to the coming *amuse bouche* of connoisseurship to excite us, even if we know we'll never savor the repast…

I have this one rule: do not attack. Let anyone harm me in any way; let them work my knees with bludgeons, brand my heels and scourge my back. If one wants to clear the world of its conventions—not add them up—there's but one choice, don't raise a hand, don't take a step. What difference if the bucket's filled with bitumen or sugar sap. Could have served as well as a spittoon...

φ

The carnage of dogmas—a state of unreality, of non-sensation. One must exceed the boundaries of archetype or paradigm, the bulwark of exigency. Custom is for everyone, but the law is for *everyone else*...

And why should I turn back in shame when taken to advantage, when on hands and knees I scratch my way from quarry to escape? Why seek absolution from a languid mob of sycophants when those who hold the purse strings are not made to pay the price? Silence and disfigurement save the sickly lamb from slaughter; let the fattened, toothsome bleaters take the first place in the chute. Show your easy inanition, the blisters on your humpback; show the sores that cut your figure gray from shattered shins to crest. Mutter incoherently and let them take a gander for as long as they can stand it—they may turn away or gloat a while, but you have always won the stare for never having lifted eyes to meet the savage glance…

φ

There is surely as much happening on the ground as at eye level. One must look down to see it, it stands to reason. But neither of these claims—both tossed off, as idle premises—does anything to interrupt the practice of doing otherwise, of refusing any notice of such ready fortune, so luxuriously appointed, so endlessly abounding in the treasures of the null. And even this assertion—a turn of phrase as fleeting as it is lively—has done little, perhaps nothing, to justify an interest in the exercise of looking only down. One must first prove that a difference has a consequence—*makes a difference*—if one expects it to be understood as more than merely novel, thus to have the least effect on the construction of a novel ground…

I am trying to be *guilty*—of such a hate that no mistake is possible. Why should *I* avoid the malice of some ardent thrust, some martial stagger? Is it not the same sort that distils *my* chary privilege? The same gloss that invigorates *my* tongue to such stale rime? So we model all of our contentments, as starving children play at being rich…

φ

If our knowledge is impugned by our attempts at profundity—our charge to plumb the hidden depths—then one is better left to ply such trade upon the surface, to scuttle the opprobrium of absence by refusing to abstract from the sum total of perceivable distinctions as a means to the discernment of the truth; by standing at the entrance to the world beyond appearance but refusing to take notice, to see past…

What a disappointment, to still be capable of disappointment…

φ

Those who are tormented by death make of dying what it will be
when it takes the form of being-dead. Freed from the fear of
dissolution, such decease in turn propitiates a fealty to the eschaton,
for which we pay the price of knowing death will never come for
us, but only for the world we're taken out of—the blank, that is to
say, we've left behind…

One conceives the aim…the very *purpose* of all action on behalf of some belief its mere *adoption*—its congruence with the commune of the dauntlessly convinced—and the presumed accord of practices that is itself identical to…*indistinguishable from* that acceptance in no way proves that such an end is better reached by revealing the importance of the distinction thus adduced *by* it, the difference whose espousal into practice brings about that—again, only presumably—desired stance…

φ

One must have first principles if one is to have seconds. That such assignment of supremacy—such an out and out *premiership* of primordial succession—is itself impossible to justify synthetically…

How unpack this hogshead of procedures and adducements, piled each upon another just as querulously guessed? Perhaps a method of some kind...a method is in order...is in the very order of... Go ahead, preach your gospel to an indifferent laity; make them stink with your compassion; and pollute their torpid aspects with deformity...

φ

The ecstatic is a state more recollected than experienced. Even when we *feel* it—when the rapture is upon us—it is still only an order of reflection, of *mimesis*; released from such unreason, we are captives to our immanence, and thereby cannot substitute the proven for the true...

What could be more obvious, could stand out more discretely from the disarray that orients this compass of encompassments to difference, to *discernment*? What could more routinely drive this aggregate of currents towards its concord in the suction of some *final* drain? The order of putrescence will serve as the horizon of our doctrine, our phronesis—that all claims to completion are established by the spoil they pass *through*...

φ

It is, so you see, the gravity of *conscience* that propitiates our interest—conceived as a repulsion that confers the weight of substance to all differential...to everything deemed knowable by cognizance of movement, of purposeful resistance; everything that's *of itself* made servant to the promise of repulsion from...But I digress, and so by definition. Even here, even now, as I fly through the air with an ease that no proficient before me has compelled into such jubilant persistence, I still can't help but trace the curve of earth that turns beneath me. Even I, that is, cannot escape the sovereign circumbendibus—the *traveling in circles*—that plays foil to all foray into guided flight...

Why risk the dejection of *nearly* winning the race by running at the front of the pack? One can lead the whole way through and still fall three feet from the finish, and those who are remembered—thus subjected to *reproof*—have broached the reckless gumption to draw nigh the pole position but still failed to overtake it, not those who merely finish in the back…

φ

That which projects its future is determined—is *distinguished*—by the pith of such projection alone. No matter what the vision or the gravity of insight, every animate entelechy is bound as both a phenotype and agent by conation *in accordance with* the prospect of discernible result. It is how that craves craves, how that shies shies; and though such universals are not usually my métier, I vouch the apodeictic when the circumstance permits—So goes meaning, so goes everything that means…

The fulcrum and the lever are all that are required to convince a studied mass to barter one pose for another, but the fealty of the onlooker who's found no easy quarter is a different story…Why *this* should be a story when the rest has hardly made the leap from sentiment to quarto, I don't precisely know. I *vaguely* know there isn't much to guzzle at the bottom of the cauldron, and what goes for gruel is true of any figurative speech…

φ

It is commonly believed that all misfortunes have their value, that every failure intimates a pathway to success. But what remains unstated is that value is progressive, that we only construe merit in the aftermath of downfall by disruption of such measure as a reference to some ideal end, thus making it coherent with the *next* presumed advance…

The burden of apperception is adduced from the mere *fact* of its assemblage—the compiling of all difference between *this* world and the last. Still one must not misconstrue some venerated venue for its infarcted contents, an idealism that follows the confusion of the visceral and the primary, the self-same and the pit of the sufficient…

φ

A quick succession of images. No time left for scribbling. Regret for the hobbled haruspex, for the vanquished Jeremiahs who first asked the question. Nothing—but the oddity of a genial humor. Genial but dry. Daubing for a guinea in a drunk tank. Confess it. It's still your lot to lose…

Tell me, finally, you've had all you can take. Say there's no point going on. Make *that* your first point...

φ

One must accept one's guilt without the means to secure punishment; to be always in the wrong, to strive to make the next *in* aptly otherwise, but always fail...A contagious acrimony, this resentment without consequence. The drones disgorged by entropy edulcorate the idols of embittered maxims. That the exception becomes commonplace, that one's passion always serves the most intractable anathemas—the void that takes tomorrow's place will stake every goodbye on new and newly binding lies, by which our bygone clomp towards this prevailing *in absentia* is invented as a failed pursuit, a *wrong* design...

The world may be decided by one's own comportment in it but that doesn't mean the *placement* that contrives it is intrinsic, that those thereby arrayed have made their strides conform to purpose—to the practice of reflection or the posture of decline. Not just anyone, that is to say, can be the sort whose lathe is turned without brooking resistance, or whose fortune is determined at the moment of expulsion from the horde...

φ

We are led to believe that the problem with consumption is scarcity, that with sufficient resources our extravagance is no cause for disdain. Such fallacy results from our attempts to limn an origin, to make the genealogy of virtue an assault against...

When everything is dead, all ends alike. So all *happens* in the dying; let the dead amuse themselves…

φ

The praxis that conveys our resolution towards inertia is intrinsic to its clearance—as a model of achievement, of a *final* final cause. The slowing of the world in the direction of its quietus is not fashioned as a deluge, nor some cleansing inundation, but seeps to fill each unattended rupture in the marl…

You can't say that you didn't have your chances, that you weren't warned. Keep in mind—it's never too late. Your time is always coming on, no matter what the present scene appears to manumit. Every demiurge finds exeunt, every field goes barren sometimes. Or better, *don't* keep it in mind. Do what you like. Perhaps *this* is just the chance *we've all* been waiting for. Yes, me too. Who would dare discharge oneself from such a fearsome troupe. Who would dare. Every mouth fills up with roots—sometimes…

φ

To have the barest influence by persiflage or argot—to think this verging rhapsody a harrow blade unblunted by the soil that receives it—one must describe the differences that bulk its eager parlance, that the premise, once adopted, will have some certain consequence, and that, dare I say, not just *any* consequence, but one that is desirable, at least more than the present state. Easier said than done, perhaps, but that doesn't mean the saying's all that easy, or the doing difficult…

And what precisely is not just as toilsome to realize? What act of dreaming parliament or wavering inquiry is not easier to say—to *describe* doing—than it is to do? Why is this a bromide I still pose for your attention, when nothing but the least of all endeavors— the drawing of the next breath after this one, or the one before— presents the varied prospect of activity less difficult to perform than to advance as an advancement *towards* performance? Does it require any lesser an expression of one's effort to say that one is saying than it does merely to say…

φ

Thus the point I've been trying to make, that I've been saying I'm going to make, which has hardly proven easier than making it— if some truism is always true, and that realization can't justify a consequent revision of behavior or intent, then why should one care if it's true or not? Why try to convince you of what's assumed by…what's *inviolable* to your nature, even if it's otherwise unknown to any trust? A question that already deems *itself* a sort of common- place, a granting of pedestrian redactions, if you like…

To plough yon rocky field one must have oxen yoked and trammeled, one must prod the restive beast to push it forward towards the verge. There is reason to presume that you will pay me no attention should I falter in my efforts to persuade you to surrender, to adopt a new position by the feint of looking down. Which requires you believe the practice helpful, if not prudent, that you somehow come to think what you have erstwhile disregarded as a pittance a new kingdom, and your wavering aversion an obeisance—to fear...

φ

In primitive relations there is little left to squander; the glutton must be outcast for the good of all the rest. But we are not such dolts, and our consumption is not measured; we take for *our* example the intemperance *of sight*...

You restrain yourself with rapture, with the dream of easy pleasures—but for what. It's not that we want different ends, that somehow we've crossed paths without a terminus in common; you'll find your way to equipoise, just like all the rest. The dispersion of doubt? No reason to pursue it. What distinguishes our method of disposing of the world is that we never found it present, that we never *thought it right...*

φ

Destiny is payback for the crime of taking chances; one does not have the courage or the cunning to turn back. Everything hurts; everything angers. Memory is a wound made by remedial assaults. It ruins everything—this press of tumid members to the tattered lips, the pinking gash. A morbid discipline, born of weakness, refuses everything, no longer reacts to anything; the vigor of defensive instinct takes on the insipid appearance of valor. To accept one's life as though it were *necessity*, to be here only what one is, the only *what* that one has ever been—this is the insult and the commerce of forbearance, the offense of the defeated. This—and all is broken, as a sword across your back...

I want to clear the world of its attachment to ruination; to leave a mark upon the arid loam where I *dig in*...

φ

The surgeon exscinds the degenerate part, and so remains a model of the salutary kind. What distinguishes the project of submission from such passion for degeneracy is that those for whom it stands as both a pennant and a marker are not merely the infected, but have spread that grim contagion to all harbors of remaining health. The instinct for denial; the ancillary decadence of nothing so much as reason, of nothing so much...

One looks down. One turns away. These are the views that survive the catastrophe, the end that's always only just begun. As yet, no reason to believe such vain deflection will return us to the portent of appearance—to our exile from all substance by injunction against predicates, against capitulation to the unity of form. In order to effect a change in the behavior of *anything*, one must in turn repudiate the inertial forces that preserve its present purchase— a slow decay that disavows each posture in its resting place, as in its final placement...

φ

To say that there is difference in the angle of occlusion—from the cocked head of the gossip to the supplicant's last bow—is hardly a great feat of wit or ratiocination, and surely doesn't rate the force of *this* sort of harangue. None of which would matter were it not for the first premise—perhaps still hidden, who can say it for themselves. I suppose any of us can, but that's of little consequence. Any of us *could* say—just flip an artful page or two...and there you have it. You've only just begun and all the answers are emerging. It's hardly past your bedtime and already you've got reason to stay wakeful through the night, to wait the dawn...

Consent is the artifice of confidence, the trick by which the swindler levels fools against their interests. If you agree to play the game, if you are willing to cheat fortune, then the guilt—the *dereliction*—is yours alone....

φ

What more can I offer; an acquisitive limpidity. Look up and be astounded, see the hackneyed modes and fashions of perfunctory salons. Passage through this labyrinth of ejecta is a life sentence. The ravaged earth sleeps...

To live with the catastrophe is to be absolved of all sins, but not through an abatement of the sanctions or anathemas by which one has been chosen for the affect of such transitive repose. To all at once assume responsibility for everything; to forgive the crimes of others by releasing them from guilt. To be an eager exile from the land grant of redemption, and so to rest, for first and last—*for once for all*—redeemed…

φ

We are searching for a praxis that eludes the metaphysics of a vulgar enthusiasm by establishing the science on the measure of the variance it presents to those who live it—or those who are securely in its grasp. If a difference makes no difference, it's unlikely to arouse its distrait audience to credence; every dogma, once accepted, takes on water like a ship's hull in a torrent, and one can't justify the trouble of the salvage if the cargo is thought useless, or the crew burgeons with gills…

The immanence of revelation—*pars pro toto*. An outcast from the rapture—the *ecstasis*—of decay...

φ

There may be other unions where the pivotal analogy—for this is, after all, an *argumentum ad analogos*—presumes a form of discord, an exit from the passage it invariably proscribes. If so it is, then so it will be; I seek neither to find it nor the stomach to adjourn. Have I not already made a practice of distancing the problem from all claims to simple verity? If it's truth you have on offer, then you might as well forget this deftless patchwork of a parody and find another rostrum from which to hawk your wares. Now, if it's truth you want to *buy*...

At last, a near return—although it seems a new digression. One can't pick up where one started and still think it bares the same face that it met when *yours* was young. That we murder to dissect may be a premise long conceded. That we disfigure to pursue…Enough. I find it difficult to reach out and contrive the feat as progress; I have nothing to give back but what is given in return. I have nothing to *succumb* to but the prospect of returning…I said—*Enough*. No reason to protect the rising river from the dam…

φ

The problem that confronts us bodies forth a certainty I'm not certain of my powers to describe with any great wit, by suggesting the avoidance of a fate I have accepted as inevitably mine—the fate of the ignored, of the unnoticed; the fate of the Cassandra who is never revealed to anyone, whose name will come to represent what it has since presented, the echo of a mutter in an empty wood. Who would ever ask for otherwise—*why do I still*…

That which stands before time cannot touch it; contiguity is only possible for those who are extended. A presence after time must contravene all sense of progress—all progression *towards* transcendence—the derogating boon of every kinship claim...

φ

Robbed of any sense of pre-existing the horizon, this play of second chances seems an escapade, a trick. Look up all you want, I say, there's nothing more to look back in remonstrance but—the plundered void, the raging blank...

And this, it seems to me, is quite enough. What do I want with your *civitas dei*; what good is such a polity to one who seeks no purchase in the sacred *or* the chastened; whose delaminated sinew always stays *so close to ground*—A dullness, a surrender, in which nothing lacks…

φ

The sovereignty of the catastrophe is always insufficient to its subjects, its *subjected*; there are those who *want in* on the action, who would jump the steepest break to feel the pressure of a shackle never taken off once fastened. To think oneself a serf within the villeinage of history is always to presume its end—its *immanent* transcendence; otherwise, nothing. Otherwise, no rant before the guillotine, no sermon from the gallows. Good enough. But why must it travel in both directions? Why must it be wanted? Why, finally, hasn't it *already happened*…

What is the world but something that *befalls* me, something that extends beyond the reach of the ostensive, however it's inscribed? What will be will not not be, or I will not become it when I manifest as what I'm ever not. What *has* been is excluded from the present last persistence of relations, of relating...

φ

It's easy to accept that speech is inadequate, but easier still to idealize silence...

Perhaps one can at least impede the scree of constant motion—the roil of an indigence still wallowing in prototype—by averaging the dissonance of this life with a picture of the next. An infinite, that is to say, not *as* you but *for* you. Me, I mean. I suppose that's understood—that I mean me by you, and that the preterit is marked by its surveillance of a world to come. By surveillance I mean—production. I suppose that's understood...

φ

Trade mouth for void—speech for asphyxia—and the kingdom of heaven inflates you, like a sail...

If one accepts that every social order signs its own apology, that one's languor in devotion to the articles of virtue is a form of preservation, adapted to its circumstance and mode, then why should one attempt to drive one's comrades from such credence? How have I been moved to waste the vim at my disposal on an end that, at its surface, seems so hapless and bemused…

φ

There are times when a false unity—a unity without restraint—assumes a place otherwise reserved for silence, for the visceral estate of flaccid organs, thus—a simulacrum of necessity. It is the gift of somber ease and swift contractions that makes such pain stand out against the lucre of preponderance, the pillage of a currency made worthless by abandoning all standard manufacture of its coin…

How much a little sun can do. Every sempiternal ache is deadened by the blinding glare, the jaundiced hue. A dullness in which nothing—no, not *even* nothing—lacks...

φ

If there is reason to fear knowledge, it's that all we know are trifles, the most frivolous of subtleties digressing towards display. No one can seem trifling and still cling to advantage; no one can *presume* to be the sum of what they claim...

The moment of the question is not passing, is not ever born of utterance. To vent the swollen cortex of discernment one must cleave the world behind the eye, the view whose only challenge to abjection is persistence. The question is—the umbral bulge, the probe that clears the pathway from horizon to deponent. The question is—the cataract of empty sighs, of open ground. Always *approaching* utterance…

φ

A life undone is a life fulfilled—a rhapsody of fragments. One succeeds against duration by surrendering to squalor, to the indolence of absence; by becoming an intruder to, or into…

Why should *I* care if *you* take on a practice that's already proved its fitness—a practice that you're only likely…only *able* to surmise by the persuasive adducement of precisely its characterization as just such an end in itself? And should my deft exertions guarantee easy accession to this policy of easement, how would I hearken to the harrowed role of avatar—one so utterly embarrassed by solicitude, let alone by supplication; one so much more comfortable *with bondage* than assault…

φ

The choice is between monstrosity and obeisance, exclusion and resentment. Anyone who's properly diseased—thereby *stricken* from all fellowship—will realize the indifference of their final objectivity, the emancipating *lassitude* of common ground…

I have tried to disregard your passion for remittance. I have tried—
but no more. You are not my only chance. I take that back. You
may or may not be my *only* chance; but you are *certainly* my last…

φ

Be assured, dear friend, I will oblige with more than courtesy; I will
give you what I can, meaning only—what I must. Such inquisitive
readers are not the common lot; I never thought I'd find myself
conferred this sort of confidence—this unrelenting *leeway*. That I,
too, would be bequeathed such indolent affection, inclusion in a
prelacy of vagabonds who—without a second thought—would
agree to sally forward with nothing but the claim that *this* peculiar
reasoning will prove more rewarding than the cull of slack intend-
ments that professes—then projects—their present course…

Some have put the best parts of their lives behind them—an enviable station. Our lives *ought* to be behind us—where they can no longer be spared…

φ

The world presents its most esteemed rewards to that sovereign whose grandeur most inspires fear—not of power, but—of absence, the image of relinquishment to sinecure, to *ruin*. It hardly needs be said that there is more attention ceded to the prating sophist than the bowed recusant, that those who'll fill the stands to watch the next auto-da-fé are now indifferent to its victim, and so that such crude impotence presumes innate requite. It hardly needs saying, but that is neither in the charter nor the deed of this profession—that what needs be said be said; that no deity survives the froward truck of incarnation; that the promise of delayed decay is only seen in effigy; and that there are more teardrops shed for loved ones who depart without the stain of recognition than for the same preceded by the florid fare-thee-well…

One must suffer without pride, without the least disapprobation. One must believe…must *come to know* that one has *always* deserved worse…

φ

There is nothing not remaindered by the portent of catastrophe; the beheadings of patricians at a vanquisher's command does little to quicken a more equitable distribution of the profits of their stratum. But at least *they* see the problem *with fresh eyes*…

Contrary to common wisdom, the unity of consequence cannot repair the fracture of the vessel that receives it, that effectuates the next inherent warrant of an end. It is easy enough to conceive oneself a substance without predicates, but only in fulfillment of a promise never understood as precedent, which is to say a promise *never made...*

φ

All signs have the same value—the value of a weakened pulse. It is this inhuman clarity that compels us to the counting...the *re*counting of discernibles, and so the immemorial retreat from sullied canvas to take stock of what the image ploughs beneath the trim of calloused blank, the cast of wounded host. Is there some discrete arcanum that relates the bourne of likeness to the burden of its calculus, of margins cut to frame the scene, the worm beneath the slough? Is the poison in the thirsty wood or in the tainted spigot? The sap runs thin, the waste runs off...

To understand one's wretchedness as fateful—as *election*—is the most egregious vanity. It may help endure the squalor, but at the price of its acceptance—of conceiving oneself boundless, in a world without bounds...

φ

No reason to look closer, to simulate detachment. Essences can only be inferred from pure sensation by first correcting for our love of balance. It's not really a subtraction, but rather an *adjustment*, as a lens repairs myopic sight, a redress *by deformity*...

If there is comfort in the prospect of one's coming incarnations, it's the comfort that the loser takes in knowing there will always be another chance to try one's luck, to place a bet…

φ

The fallacy of possession is the claim that it's one-sided, that the predicate pays homage to the subject that suborns it, and so that no such tribute can be measured as result. The imperative of character is kin to its transmission, but only insofar as the malady of *characterization* is incurable…

Situated just beyond the hold of singularity, the consolation of the eternal is its standing as a deficit, as an aggregated *loss*. That this peculiar recourse to self-evidence claims to manifest as object— is surrendered *to the genitive*—is what at once distinguishes such referent from its meaning, what sunders every meaning *from its drifting off…*

φ

I'm sure you will agree that I am not without my standards; not a subject to desire in my motives and complaints, but rather in the way that my responses suborn answers, and my answers serve to catalyze every next step as retreat. Having placed myself outside of all such surreptitious compass—even that proved by *suggestion* of my seeming distance from it—I feel some sort of duty to this frenzy of demurrals, a burden that requires such inceptive divagation from the form of divagation…

Neither abandoned nor companioned, neither gifted nor received, the time has come to part with everything—I can take in nothing more. Surmise is still not purchase; no one wants their appanage of bile to congeal. No one speaks *my* name, it's true, but then you have to realize—I, of *all* your creatures, have not *earned* a name...

φ

The catastrophe is indifferent, but no less predisposed. The imperium of longing, the emergence of...

By silence I made myself echo, by digging I made myself sward; to be prodigal in one's renunciations is to presume that one is listening to someone...to something not assaultive, but still animus by form. The slightest sway of drunken breeze, the sudden hesitation of the mob—we learn our lessons. Always semblant, always finding in the fractional *a sum*...

φ

Declaim in proper sequence every suppliant effect, the completion of a life lived in resistance to pursuit...

It's not only for the fact that I'm above all such discernment of impediments and bounds, but that this vague discrepancy is itself the only means to effectuate distinction from superfluous regard. To suggest that *re*cantation still insinuates a claim is already to make subtraction of the thing itself from any understanding of *thingness* impossible, replacing the principle of sufficient reason with an acceptance of its failure, its inherent lack. That such admission may still find itself beholden to some forfeiture intrinsic *to its own* nature is not surprising, but for all that it compels this disquisition no step further towards its imminent internment—or its next release…

φ

The glib heresiarchs pay tribute, now that we've ransomed their tongues. They make every concession, so to gain their fated lethargy, to hear their song of freedom thus unsung from its requital, from the need to make their perquisite of suppliance a common share, a bargain won…

No conscience is made servitor to its unique persistence, its median forced front against inexorable decline. It's not the slumping vizard that wears the shape of insufficiency, but the sense of its possession, of each novel balance pressed into the clutch of ruptured frame. One who would think otherwise is not derelict, perhaps, but dissuaded from a fealty to their own condign essentia is abandoned at first entrance, on their ingress of a way. They may forgo all knowledge of corporeal momentum for the tilt of anamnesis, may swallow every punitive adducement to concede to idle parlance in support of idle scheme, but that is nothing when compared to this impenetrable discharge from the burden of agency, the infinite leisure of *being superfluous*...

φ

Where no one's ever been, where there's nothing to hold onto; where one can pierce the skin with mere caresses and, delivered out of prattle, speak one's rank conciliation with a chorus of groans. As if *that* were a beginning, or an end begun...

To a person they boast of their rights—by which they mean their privileges. One need but suffer through the masquerade of subjugation to make all the world protectorate. They want what they're denied—and nothing more...

φ

As if the close towards which this queer monography is lurching is equal to the conquest of its mover's voice within it. As if one is only able to identify a crossroads if one holds with equal certainty that somewhere there's an omnibus on which that pass is limned...

I would happily do something else, forgo this seeping pellicle of counterparts and pretenses for some communal office, some remunerative post; who *wouldn't* want for more than this…this… *this*…if they only had a choice—if they had *ever* had a choice…

φ

There are, in the end—the beginning of the end as at its middle or its finish—more than enough exits for the traveler too weary to continue—portals, if you will, into the reveries of many other equally agreeable departures and distractions, diversionary tactics that can bring the task to term. There is gathering abundance just behind the copse that walls you in, just abaft a branch or two, it's yours for the taking and…And what difference *to you* if all your doorways are mirages? Does the *illusion* of the ordure in your gullet taste sweeter than its presence? Or the dream from which one never wakes provision its prone omphalos with something less than *bona fide* emissions? And if one gazes out upon the anodyne remonstrance of some far flung *ignis fatuus*, what difference that the vapor takes its lumen from some otherwise unknowable enchantment—or *decay*…

Virtue is contrived to mask—and thereby to *confirm*—the need of reason to coagulate around its absent aggregate before it can find means to the surrender of its due. We all stand as fulfilled by standing-in, by interregnum; to cede even *this* throne is to abandon us to duty, and so return to sovereignty by giving up one's will...

φ

You are just as much a prisoner as I am, or...no...I am just as much as you are. That's right. Just as much as you. But—who said *you* had to be here? Who gave *you* permission *to lock yourself in*...

When I look about me with the wide eyes of a sallow youth—the youth that I draw ever closer to surviving with each novel suppuration of this calloused howl, this raucous boast—I find a bulge of lineaments made visible by trains of milky mirrors, the weight of a celestial husk that stumbles and balks like a donkey at every turn; I accept the new horizon that each squint across the shroud of bluing oculus presents as though a challenge, a supple lack that tempts me to the succor of illimitable stour. I find the measured carcass of the measured void, and wonder where the rest is, where they've hidden the remainder…

φ

When I look about me—a peculiar enough notion. Have I not already said as much, declared myself the first…the *only* oligarch impelled to claim the proceeds of such regulative blinding? Have I neglected to suggest I've given myself over to a policy distinguished by *privation* of pursuit? That I've lived another par and found it lacks the shine—the proper *luminance*—to flower and to ripen? Have I asked of my admirers the names of their crimes? Of their *constituents*, even? Who else, in the final days, will quaff this cunning vintage? Who else press this noble rot, these shriveled vines…

The child's eyes betray us. Everything lingers past its use. One finds vestiges of fairy tales on shopping lists. Prophetic murmurs sough from every roadside gulch. When one discerns the moment through its *coming* recollection, the haze clears. One knows how it will seem to have lost *this* time. What one will someday make of something so much *less* than memorable; the pain of a loose tooth; a glint on the sea...

φ

Desire—for those who've come to it by bequest—can only be suspended through its infinite deferment, its replacement with the proxy—the *succedaneum*—of compulsion...

I am not one of many, nor am I one of a kind, but I *am* many…

φ

There is no one better suited to the office of redeemer than the haruspex of slaughter, the siren of affliction preaching poison brood to brood. It is *for* that fated catalyst that the history of failure is constructed as a preterit, but *by* it almost nothing new is settled or revealed. Which is precisely what contrivance of a history amounts to; the *putting off* of agency as votive alms to eschaton, the end of all our suffering by suffering…

What place did you *expect* within the order of causation? Did you
think that you—pitying, insentient you—were a more likely impera-
tor of archetypes and persuasions? That such a presbyopic could
receive the world as cover from the shelter of its view? Is it the
promise of plunder that keeps you lurching through this march-
land? Did you think *you* were the agent of *your own* abandon, that
I was simply put here as an escort or a guide? History, worse still, is
the occupation *before the conquest*, the subjection that preponderates
beyond and against the catastrophe...

φ

The interior convocation of the ego requires that all vacancies
be filled. Thus one is precluded from the unalloyed delirium of
signifying nothing by the capital propinquity of wholeness, of
consenting to live only as a oneself...

Whether appetite for mastery or hunger for sensation, the only truly *profitable* vice is one that vitiates our interest in its object, that rejects what we have longed for at the moment it's received…

φ

Absolve from further censure the oracular ebullience that enlivens the anemic casuist—that's what I say. It may appear an apothegm most furtively self-serving, which is hardly a distinction of note in the course of this adventure; it is, after all, what qualifies epigrammatic speech—that it serve its humble speaker in a way never availed the prosy narrator of conscience or the sorcery of broken-lined caesurae. If I thereby paint with a stroke too broad to draw with proper detail, so be it. One may well cut a twig with a butter knife, *but an oak needs an ax*…

There is no easy comfort in the groan across the floorboards, no reason to feel settled when awaked from nervy drowse, which is why all those of faith do as the imbecile Reformer, attributing each creak to some loosed devil in carouse. And knowing no perversion of the godhead could do *us* harm, we return to the election of a sound sleep...

φ

To retire from conviction one must turn away from judgment, from all interest in correction *or* surmise...

It's difficult for me to think you've made it this far—*even* this far, leaving so much ground to cover with the shadow of an ant—if the project couldn't exculpate the efforts of your balance, the votary communion such excursus has advanced. And so the boiling over of this mulligan stew can hardly seem more insult than the fool's broth of credulity, and that without requiring the dinner guests to bring a spoon, to take a sip...

φ

They have the courage to fight for their truth, but lack the intellect to challenge it. They are, perhaps, *happy*...

To convict the merry dabblers of collusion *against* agency; to open them up, as it were, while always turning towards the strata. To alert the vatic lushes to the mire of arrears in which they languish, in which they see the promise of their future joys; this is the telos that distinguishes catastrophe from antiphon, that ensures the supplication of all vision *to its ground*...

φ

No reason to lurch forward, to go looking for an ending. It may be true this memoir only lasts a single page, but it's a page without a back side, or a margin...

Character consists neither in feeling for others, nor in taking aim at such remonstrance—not in thrusting one's perdurable relation to transcendence into open view—but in enduring the gradual discernment of one's own lapsed nature, the amity of *being-with* in what amounts to mutual decay. That such depleted hunting grounds yield little more than forage does not seem a defect, or rather, it's just the sort of defect that purposes such toil to advantage…

φ

Nor is it the case that isolation is desirable; sometimes one feels compelled to seek it, sometimes it appears as a privation to be filled. It's not that *being pleased* bespeaks of quality or content; such pose is still excluded from the purview of the present cull. Rather, it's this *absence* of quality—this winnowing of caries from the shape of every pose—that holds the fractious vestiges of character in relation to our axial attempts at self-inscription, the guaranteed rebuff of one's embrace of humankind…

We sense we'll be removed by some disaster—but we don't know which one. It keeps us pressing forward, keeps us thinking of new answers; our interest in the posture of our final degradation is the means by which we bear the wait, the failure to move…

φ

Had I found a way to circumvent this mire of interstices, I would not have attempted to go over it; had I prevailed in going over it, I would not have begun to dig…But that's the point. Avoid the path of least resistance from the outset. Every hillock holds the option of a *tunneling beneath*…

One is not *always* excluded—which is to say that sometimes one's exclusion *is a choice*...

φ

The fragment finds its place within a general structure, no matter whether such design is patent or unseen. That you look for possibilities where there are none, that you turn your back on every opportunity that comes your way as though it were a pittance of a future share—a promised sheen—is neither reason to reject your hand nor some form of delay. You are what you have always been—the best I could have hoped for—and let us leave it... whatever it, whichever what...at that...

Attentive stealth requires one exist only externally. In order to create the self one must first destroy all others. And to destroy the self? What other obligation can impart sufficient reason to the world...

φ

The path fills in, foundations crumble. The cicatrix recalls the form of implement by which the wound is fixed within its purling lips, the kernels of resemblance whipping frenzied fruits from modal pips. One must put one's faith in dullards who with measured wits insist they sight the sightless line, that there upon the ruffled schists of summits seeming merely to consist of indiscernible erosions is a hidden byway waiting for the rationed hoofs of pilgrims to reveal the steps—the paling steps—of workman long deceased. How they know their way about such furtive bounds I won't presume to guess, but that is neither relevant nor motive to resist; I have confidence in many things that still remain obscure for my disinterest or my nescience, it couldn't matter which...

As much as it appears that prayer is possible in common, the deity hypostatized by iterative orison is only made approachable to individuals—to those whose cloying dispatch is born of solitude. It is *this* act of selection that excludes all proper servants from such service to a sovereign, such tributary passion; this that makes such sovereignty an *impotent* rebuke…

φ

If conviction were itself enough to discharge one's existence— if one could rest assured it's better to have *not* been, and by that realization cease abiding in duration, in the amiable present of what will surely prove some future pain—then the reason for persistence would rest in our attempts at such assurances, the possibility of making the world vanish in the cogito. So would the idea of good replace the good, and mere existence—at long last premised into predicate—stimulate the godhead—at long last proven into presence—to at long last disappear…

Barred from understanding innovations made quotidian, one re-monstrates against such adventitious techne and its corresponding premises while still expecting it to buttress one's most comforting effects...

φ

There is nothing so consoling as the diminishment of self; the substance of the world that we inhabit may prove metaphor for something that has never existed—whose existence is a lie, if not construed as a mistake—but nonetheless the measure of our interaction with it is the endlessly retributive contraction of its middle, of its *inner* pitch...

In consequence of treating one's emergence into seity as though it were completed, one is startled by the portion of one's carcass that recoils from its outline, as the withering contractions of a salted slug. Thus the stake of apperception is the thinking into spirit of a self at once made mutable by thinking through...

φ

The power of a moral idea is a measure of the extent to which we think it counterfactual—to which, that is, it seems to contravene our present course. No matter our collations into dissonant communions or our tearful recrudescence to the piecework of campestral versts, the world will not spin faster on its axis, or take a different slant in its career across the vault...

There is something rendered possible—at the least secured—by the propaedeutic of persuasion, and that only made manifest by our avoidance of—our *return from*—the depletions and discomforts of its voluble collapse. That one might well experience this absence of diminishment as a form of augmentation—might perceive the motion of the waves as an assault against the presumed stability of some tossing skiff—is neither surprising nor of interest. What matters is that something...that *anything* happens; that anything has ever had the slightest *chance* of happening, whether or not it's happened yet...

φ

Know that one must languish in deferral of contentment; that one will only find a home in exile from all *ease of acceptance*...

To concern oneself with history—a fixation as deplorable as its object is absurd. In order to conceive the tale, one must live its horizon; in order to describe the world, one must make claims beyond…

φ

So go the aesthetes about their business—and what do *you* do. They dig; you praise the rigor of their ditches. They keen; you laud the virtues of lament. And suddenly—it's you. It's *your* disfigured portrait that appears so foul and feckless. Suddenly you see yourself—and what. Isn't it enough to make you sleep again? To force your idle talons into softer skin? Don't you, like all the rest, still dream your fitful welter a divergence from your wallow in…

One wants to be relieved of every last responsibility—would like a fresh start, a new hold on the tenuous collapse of a tenuous resistance. One desires nothing so much as a thrashing, an *acknowledgement* of the failure of one's attempted escape. Only then can one rest easy, can one escape the question—*escape from what...*

φ

To manifest the same duress—the same depleted exigence—that draws the languid servitor to empty glass...

One wants, that is, to take a gulp *and have one's glass refilled.* That such desires are impassioned in inverse proportion to their satisfaction is hardly a great insight. That our love of freedom—our aversion to imprisoning fulfillments, of fulfillments *in principia*, if you will—is our dearest concession to bondage, well…

φ

Rain speaks in glossolalia. Wets the appetite for run-on sentences. Those who have dropped their throats must pick them up with damp leaves. Corruption is a danger, but—one's hands are always tainted. Who can help it; who would *want* to—that's the prize…

In order to free ourselves, we must be rid of all enthusiasms. The project is laborious, but then we realize—we cannot rid ourselves of our enthusiasm for freedom…

φ

Perhaps you are but one of many stalwart undecideds, perhaps you *play* the middle part but teeter on the brink. I suppose there is no reason to blame any individual for a weakness that's been leading the decline of humankind for centuries. But you're not just *any* individual…

I may not have anything to give you on the order of such fungible esteem—or to take away from that succession, regardless of your present line. One can't presume the one without the other; if it's significant to you that you've been granted my affections, then withholding said assurance must be taken for a lack…

φ

And what can I know of you and yours, of all your pretenses and masks? You may have noticed that we've never met, that you're no more likely to salute me on the strand than I am to look up and notice your greased trotter as you pass. What distinguishes *you* from so many other faceless dreamers dreaming trippingly of easement? What makes *your* disguise so much more difficult to see through—and take off…

Must I be the one to say it? Must one always importune the recognition of one's surrogates? Thus the most salient of your many ineluctable charms; you're now here, here now, *aren't you…*

φ

That someone else went searching for a rhapsody of action and found only this debris of shrill remonstrances and paradigms is neither my trial nor yours; there are any number of ways to pleasure oneself, as I'm sure you're well aware. That said, most such approbation in the dank sump of satiety results in little more than protestations of disservice, than the rut of dreamless sleep run down to petulant repose. A strange enumeration that claims *little more* as nothing, that counts endless repetition as the portent of return…

How release oneself from the burden of disgust? By exalting weakness, by refusing to divert from the peculiar…

φ

It may be true that nothing dies, but everything that can be said to fear fears dying most. A treacherous smile, then…surrender to persistence, to the solace of an *aimed* decease…

Let the girders rust the mortise and the shovels raze the frame.
Let the drains plug up with silt and so much colorful detritus stuff
the nuclei of armatures left out to cure. Let the craters fill with
ruptures of replete avoirdupois, and dredged of every purity leech
damp cremains into the beds of limpid rills, the parturition of this
pledged morass at last—*achieved*, if nothing else, if nothing…

φ

To begin the catastrophe is…to begin *with* the catastrophe. Such
equivoque is nonetheless not purely analytic, but made necessary
by the possibility—the very *thought*—of the catastrophe…

One longs not for the cure, but for the joys of convalescence...

φ

When all the other cities die, when all the other cities fade, there comes a time to build again, to make sure that the long deferred awakening of revenants proceeds to orderly surmise, that robbed of all their heresies the apostolic doyens train their followers to seize the dearth, to pluck the pupils from dead eyes. Those haggard wraiths, reduced to proper indigence and sized to fit a growing lack, will have so much to do before the day begins, before the shouldered burden of their labor can start giving back to sinking ground the farrow of loose humus as compacted streets, as shriven tracks, that we may never know their contributions to the balance, as an image of the muffled gust that starts the wave can't be derived from survey of the pounding surf...

By now I feel quite certain that no promise will suffice you; that you are no more likely to accept the gift of empty oaths than I am to repudiate their use. Did you recognize...did you even *suspect* there was an argument to be parsed from the preceding maxims? Did it seem to you that I was *pulling one over*, as it were, or were you ready to move on? Did you understand the passage thus considered *as* a passage—as a sleight-of-hand transition, a distraction, *a delay*...

φ

One need not know the end is certain in order to believe that it is just. Take any patent sovereignty or easy supplication for a new world and a new day, do penance as you must do, you won't find a single reason to surrender to the commerce of *discernible* results. One asks, that is, for absences made present—the *completion* of the void, not its rebuke...

There are certain investigations—certain *terms* of analysis—an analysis of which allows the musculature of reason to lurch forward towards transcendence. *Towards*, I say. A queer qualification, but there you have it. One must counter one's proclivity to authorize each portent of advancement as a *terminus ad quem*...

φ

There are, that is to say, certain moments of discrete equivocation—of return to endemic principle—that by dint of simple scrutiny force the consciousness thus energized to achieve a novel prospect, to wake up blind to the occlusion of *first* view. That such practice is on offer here or at some future juncture only figures as important if it's been distinctly proven; until this consideration of methodology adduces its object—returns to a description of its practice and the practice of its proof—one can do little but *suppose* the supplication of its speaker, the delirious implicature of the things themselves...

The mistaking of position for person is no more than a confusion of effects and causes, of things and the abstractions of their forms. It is equally misguided—and perhaps of far more consequence—to *deny* any relation between substance and its placement, between semblance and its infinite deferral to surround...

φ

Visions claimed are visions lost; one must take comfort in the fact that somewhere halfway round the world the nebulous contagion that defiles the sirocco will settle in the stillness of some abiotic hydrosere, and so at last find *form* within the muck...

Perhaps there's more than one such lemma posed without illation; if so it is, then so this ever secondary audit will reflect. Of course, if *this* were true, then there would be no need to say it, and I could well have bartered all such withering prognosis for a reckoning of details—thereby hastened to the prospect of the proof...

φ

To satisfy the judgment of the dead—a categorical compulsion. We cannot join the caravan of history without loading up our litters and our tinder carts with corpses, without dragging our dead with us, and forcing *them* to rule...

Ordinary crimes do not concern us. We are searching for the guilt of an *inexpiable* resolve...

φ

It's not enough to understand that one has been defeated, to accept with sullen certitude one's life as such a faltering collation of attempts. One must concede all options, renounce all possibilities. No wallow in the broken will can supervene the pleasure of achieved capitulation, of surrender fixed before the war, before a move against...

As though the idea of a thing were enough of a thing to ensure—
to prove *by demonstration*—the existence of *things*...

φ

That this organon of endings is no comfort or amusement I
have no doubt. That there is some aesthetic it would serve us to
remainder does not mean we are less likely to believe we ought
believe it, though this is in itself the hinge of no decisive course.
That such tremulous reflection goes no further towards transcen-
dence than the aforementioned promise of a movement towards
transcendence—now *that's* a remonstration one can sink one's
glossa into, one can fit within one's bursa, like a scarab, or a
groat...

While living *past* one's quarter in the prison of locution, one cannot ever rid oneself of having lived *within* it for a time…

φ

There are idioms and passwords, there are shibboleths and tokens, there is jargon used for rank deceit and lingo meant to cozen those who don't deserve a second glance, perhaps even a first. I've found no way to push the world past all delineation; that there's ever been a failed attempt is not my claim to prove. That there have only been such failed attempts…

The absurdity of self-interest dissolved into the effort to control the flux of tremors through stiff digits—this is the triumph of ataxia, the promise of a future made subordinate to impotence, thus an apathy impossible to yield to, or reverse…

φ

Torn between nothing—and *nothing at all*. One cannot do every-thing, no one can do everything, not if one has hopes of traveling some byway from its middle to its finish, of ending one's progres-sion to the end of one's progression…

Why anyone would hearken to such confidence, I'm not quite sure. Perhaps we have no other choice…only hold such *faith*, that is, because we think we have no other choice, accepting that such incidental credence takes reversion to its subject as a form of apologia, so releases it from differential terms. There is something in the nature of all consequent obeisance to bounds that is intrinsic to the promise of exception, of ecstasis; something that establishes a posture without standing, without status or provenience. Something that proves sovereign—*in a kingdom of ends…*

φ

Destroyed by easy pleasures, it's survival that betrays us, that makes of every history a dilettante's abandonment of vision, then resolve. We must start again. We must start again. The repetition soothes us. And this time we're aware of our affection for advantage, our fealty to position; this time we attend to the *corruption* of our wants…

Perhaps you understand that my objective in pursuing such regression—such regression to the maxim, to the precept, as a point—has as much to do with wanting to *suggest* a fateful project as it does with such a project as it presently embarks. And how to tell the difference? That's the *potestas clavium*, if you will, which only *I* possess, right here in my waistcoat pocket. Or did I leave it in my breeches' fall…

φ

The certainty of genius is the certainty of nature. The certainty of nature is—*abuse*…

To impart by endless recapitulations of my own paresis; surely
I'm not the first to fake abhorrence at such seminal abandon, to
pretend to find no solace in surrendering to fate. And surely not
the last to thus declare myself an oracle, in a world without voice…

φ

The pleasure of judgment starts at home. The first time one con-
fronts the mere *suggestion* of malfeasance, one is forced into the
ardor of moral superiority, even if its alter is an image *of oneself*…

There is cause for your suspicion, if I read you correctly—or rather, if you read *me* at all, a proposition that stands quite apart from any estimation of *correctness*, but is no less definitive for that. If you feel a bit uneasy with my boundless vim and vigor—my infinitely bounded *absence* of a proper rest—then perhaps you're not so bad after all. Which is only to suggest that I am willing to make manifest precisely what the practice of my artistry surrenders, the propulsion of my suitors towards the ends that such antipathy —my surfeit of preponderance—prevents me from attending to… *arriving at*, no matter what the stature, or the vow of such untold recourse…

φ

It is only for this purpose that I let your world pass by without so much as a citation; to *this* end you've been treated to so many failed attempts—so much undaunted emprise adumbrated by ellipsis, then omission, then the growing blank…

Perchance it takes the form of a certain convulsion, a bulge that holds the redolence of rotting flesh. One was tempted to the scene by the bloody wrists, but no one would expect the head to twitch in silent anguish from its perch in wicker basket. It is indeed a grand release, an *incomparable* frolic—the bargain of an epoch made to yoke its fetid congress to a spasm in the back of the throat...

φ

Such assumption being—the sooth of the catastrophe; the nearness—the near *terminus*—of all that it *distracts*...

If something better comes along…but what have I to do with it. I require no consistency of partisans to make my word a contract, to secure some sort of quotient of applause for my misgivings. It's why all this *works*, why this fabrication of horizons *floats*, as it were, regardless of its ballast, a voice ordained to truss its throat before the caste of character *sets in*…

φ

In this way I've become—I have *pulled myself back into*—the vertex of an ineluctable sanctification; I have made myself holy by projecting that nullity immediately precedent to holiness, the vacuum that reciprocates the dispositional abhorrence of the cosmos limned *in toto* by swallowing its deluge of exigencies; by dispersing its privation like confetti at a conqueror's parade…

To grieve for one's own forthcoming diffusion into nullity seems a reasonable—if unreasoning—regression to defensive cause, but only insofar as one claims substance in similitude, in the upraising of character as archetype, one's immutable redaction of putrescence as a final form…

φ

One finds traces of great fires in spent matches. One's heart aches with the hunger—*to destroy*…

The possibility of the world ensures its actuality. Thus the fallacy of metaphysics—that the ontology of the transcendent is secured by application of this one and only instance of such generative discernment to some…to *any* stopgap of noetic intuition, prepending the materiality of the universal from our *prima facie* decadence, the timbre of a trill that's never heard…

φ

The sooth of the catastrophe—as though the repetition of the phrase could *make it mean*…

No day bears relation to the last. No coming change of scenery can dress the wound of certitude; the cancer of decision is not remedied by mastering the labyrinth of such vain deceits. Some may think a temperate life the most effective nostrum for what ails us, but it only ever works for those who've tried another path. For the rest of us, there is no end to rancor, to the pain of parturition. For the rest of us, the world has always snuffed the spark of witness from the causal surge, the final chance...

φ

Yield to the charm of catastrophe—the climax of a certain convulsion; this is your opening to the new way, this is the new way inside the old. Retreat in step with common faith, the topos of a certain void can't hold you back, can't see you through. This is what you *can* do, what your prolix path to dispatch ever forces from the welter; this is where your triumph lies, don't doubt it...

What cannot waken cannot keep watch over dreams; only when a dreamer is not sleeping can their decadence begin. As soon as we *desire* the catastrophe, repose within its unending approach is all that's left us…

φ

When finally the first voice feigns an amiable credence, the second can assume the disposition of intent. Thus the innate principle—the empirical concession—of any crude idealism proved credulous in practice, but suspect as a dogma whose demurrer is not asked. Such principle being—such *critique requiring*—a starting point—an *actual*—from which one might progress to face the threshold of deduction, the bourne of any method whose necessity is meted out in harmony with what the claim to certainty presents. Who plays lead and who plays second—now *that's* a different story, perhaps a minor episode, but surely not…

One does not *master* silence, one *transcribes* it…

φ

When finally we notice that the predicable nature of any stock desideratum is a quantitative measure—a measure of the depth of our response to its release—we can no longer endure acts that have a specific object. This is not the same as declaring an armistice, as impotent combatants throw their hands up for effect. This is not an admission of failed performance. It is, rather, to assimilate what is clear from even the most puerile of perspectives—that desire is a ratio dissolved by its equivalence, a thrust cleared from the strata by a leveling of surfaces; that wanting is made semblable by suffering assemblage, a pouring forth that *inundates* the singular…

Our absence is *why* we want; our presence is the means by which the wont of want is thwarted…

φ

If I were silent I'd hear nothing. No time for inflection. If the pauses are not endless, then they have not really happened. What right have I to stop even a moment? Only the dead have rights, but there are other forms of warrant…

We have forgotten everything in order to see—but we don't see. We see only what we want to see—but we want to see everything. Seeing what we want, we see nothing that we want. We see nothing—but we don't see…

φ

And what could be the source of such an unrelenting confidence? How have I achieved such a conclusory persuasion without any sort of striving, any movement to dissimulate or represent the same? Such quizzical bequest propels me forward from this concourse towards an end perhaps quite disparate from the pose that any simpering denial after principle suggests; an end at once contrived to suit surveillance without witness, at least as much to do with the sufficiency of reason as it does with *making sense*…

Propinquity grows venomous when challenged—when not recipro-cally adduced. It is reason enough to agree with everything—to accede to everyone—but that is not *our* problem. How could anyone but *you* complete the confidence, the aggregate of…

φ

My viceroy indecision, made the principle of service, as the weed seeks its last nutriment within the poisoned stream. A vegetal impulse, less act than actuality, a consequence at once made both inchoate and condition for the world to come…

There is no behind to the image that conflates the world with substance, with the silence of substance; that the vestiges of voice remain indentured to the project of elision makes of every ear an address, but only for those speakers who have managed to divulge it, who have opened to the promise of *their own* excise…

φ

As a rag tossed in the street, my song portends…

Afterword
        by Brandon Brown

Steven Seidenberg's *plain sight* is a book for our grim present.
Practices of seeing have hypertrophied and made surveillance so
omnipotent it's become routinized. But *plain sight* does not leverage
the language of cable news and social media. Rather, the language
of *plain sight* addresses the present tense in a rhetoric—and with a
vocabulary—more suited to a distant past century. Yet the setting
of the book is the here and now: the time when capital is not just
late but overdue, having wasted our world enough that we not only
abide under dire forecast but can begin to witness the opening
notes of earth's decline and death. Having been offered these bad
optics, our attitude towards life despite them is to some degree up
to us…

plain sight isn't simply a catalog of the ways in which the optical fails
our desire to make the world coherent, knowable. The meaning of
seeing in this text is at stake, not assumed. Seidenberg's book lever-
ages our common (ableist) metaphor which translates "sight" as
"understanding." It's an old metaphor in Indo-European languages
and one the people who speak them have used for millennia. Just
consider how we use the phrase "I see" to indicate we get it. It's
almost always used to refer to something conceptual rather than a
simple indicative. Seidenberg's book narrates the emotional duress
of living through the opaque conjunction where cognition meets
vision meets language…

> "The moment of the question is not passing, is not ever
> born of utterance. To vent the swollen cortex of discern-
> ment one must cleave the world behind the eye, the view

whose only challenge to abjection is persistence. The question is—the umbral bulge, the probe that clears the pathway from horizon to deponent. The question is—the cataract of empty sighs, of open ground. Always *approaching* utterance..."

A stanza picked at random: the prose of *plain sight* is a running river of intense negativity, its bile and outrage hearkening to a classical vitriol. Seidenberg has included a glossary for the wild range of philosophical and other more obscure terms that distribute through the text, but even the book's "ordinary" language partakes of a vocabulary not just expansive in terms of its range but tunneled into the particular history of English. In this passage, as in much of the book, the efficacy of visibility for knowledge is scrutinized and constantly refused. However much we might want to master the book's stanzas, as with any other material object, *plain sight* unfolds in a "cataract of empty sighs..."

It's unusual for a proper *screed* to be so indeterminate. If you're writing a polemic, you typically take pains to make your targets clear. This book's bone structure is outrage, but its antagonists are hard to name. If it clearly aims its negativity at unspecific "vanquishers," it nevertheless indicts us as the subjects who accept, are complicit in, even seem to enjoy our bondage. Seidenberg scrupulously evades identification through narrative, vehemently taking up positions only to discard, dismiss, contradict them. Even the poem's form reiterates this underlining inconstancy. The book is written in paragraphs, the graphemic shape of a complete thought made of multiple propositions, but each one rejects conclusion. They all end in ellipses...

plain sight, in this formal and philosophical texture, hearkens to Nietzsche as a primary source, both in its hyperbolic emanation of negative feeling and its commitment to undecidability. As in Nietzsche, the world presented in *plain sight* offers hope, even ecstasy, inside of the general horror of our condition. I take it back—"hope" is too simple an affect for this book. I guess what I mean is this book says yes occasionally in its relentless catalog of nos. If at times it veers into nihilism ("There is no next beginning not beginning in the middle; no image of transcendence, tracing shadows in the desert..."), the book occasionally offers us a glimpse of something better, if not redemptive. Even Nietzsche writes about the imperative to lift up yourself *and* your neighbor...

I guess that situation informs how we might think, with *plain sight,* about what we can and can't elevate from experience to understanding and utterance. Naturally, ideology flourishes by impeding articulation. To hearken to an example from everyday life in the USAmerica, body and dash cameras have not really changed the murderous practices of ordinary pigs, despite the "truths" they portray. We can't believe our eyes. We would need a new definition of the visible. Or, as Seidenberg writes, "There is nothing not remaindered by the portent of catastrophe; the beheadings of patricians at a vanquisher's command does little to quicken a more equitable distribution of the profits of their stratum. But at least *they* see the problem *with fresh eyes...*"

Of course, the obvious fact that we can't access is a common enough theme in literature. "The Purloined Letter" by Edgar Allan Poe is an emblematic version. The great feat of vision performed by Dupin is to see what's in clear view, an accomplishment none of his peers could attain. And while "The Purloined Letter" is probably

a more natural reference for the excoriative tone of *plain sight,*
I draw your attention to Robert Iscove's 1999 film *She's All
That.* In *She's All That,* Freddie Prinze, Jr. plays Zack, a recently
dumped high school god, the class president everyone is dying to
fuck. He makes a bet with his jackass friend that he can make any
girl in the school prom queen. The girl selected is Laynie, played by
Rachel Leigh Cook. Laynie is an antisocial art freak, incidentally
with horrible eyesight. The task seems insurmountable...

But Zack makes strides. With the help of his sister Mac, played by
Anna Paquin, they persuade Laynie to change her hair, makeup, and
style. They throw away the clunky glasses and painter's smock,
exchanging them for eyeliner and expensive dresses. Without her
glasses, Laynie enters the universe of *plain sight:* deprived of clear
vision, she generates a new perspective, more rich and arguably
more brutal. Zack falls in love with Laynie not just for her revised
visual appearance. Laynie's confidence, eclectic taste, and spirit have
made Zack more vulnerable, giving him cause to doubt the easy
course his life had always taken, and consequently more power and
autonomy over his own future. By the end of the film, he's fully
able to tell his dad he doesn't want to go to Dartmouth. It sounds
small, but it's really everything. In being able to see Laynie, Zack is
able to see himself, or, in Nietzsche's terms (quoting Pindar), Zack
"became who he was." He was right there, all along. In comparison,
Laynie's makeover is minimal. There is something of this promise
in *plain sight...*

She's All That, like many other great works of art, thematizes our
constant failure to witness what should be easiest to register,
what's right in front of us. Similarly in *plain sight,* where all the
other senses are finally subjected to this same castigating scrutiny.

Seidenberg writes,

"There are, in the end—the beginning of the end as at its
middle or its finish—more than enough exits for the trav-
eler too weary to continue—portals, if you will, into the
reveries of many other equally agreeable departures and
distractions, diversionary tactics that can bring the task to
term. There is gathering abundance just behind the copse
that walls you in, just abaft a branch or two, it's yours for
the taking and…And what difference *to you* if all your
doorways are mirages? Does the *illusion* of the ordure in
your gullet taste sweeter than its presence? Or the dream
from which one never wakes provision its prone omphalos
with something less than *bona fide* emissions? And if one
gazes out upon the anodyne remonstrance of some far
flung *ignis fatuus*, what difference that the vapor takes its
lumen from some otherwise unknowable enchantment—
or *decay*…"

Glossary

ab ovo (ab **oh**-voh; Latin, *ab* from, *ovo*, ablative of *ovum*, egg) : from the beginning

ad absurdum (ad ab-**sur**-d*uh*m; Latin, *ad* to, *absurdum* absurdity) : as used in *reductio ad absurdum*, a method of disproving an argument by demonstrating the absurdity (or counterfactual nature) of its consequences, or proving an argument by showing its negation does the same

adit (**ad**-it; Latin *aditus*, past participle of *adire*, to approach) : a horizontal (or nearly horizontal) entrance to a mine, for access or drainage

alterity (awl-**ter**-i-tee; Late Latin, *alteritās*, otherness) : the quality or state of being different, or perceived as different

ambuscade (**am**-b*uh*-skeyd; French *embuscade*, to ambush) : an ambush

anodyne (**an**-*uh*-dahyn; Greek *anōdunos*, free from pain) 1. capable of eliminating pain; soothing 2. insipid, bland

anschluss (**ahn**-shl*oo*s; German, from *anschliessen*, to join) : a political union or annexation, often used to evoke the annexation of Austria by Germany in 1938

antiphon (**an**-t*uh*-fon; Late Greek, plural of *antiphōnon*, responsive) 1. a line or verse sung responsively 2. a rejoinder of any kind, including any phenomenon determined an effect—symbolic or mechanical—in its relationship to cause

appanage (**ap**-*uh*-nij; Old French, *apaner*, to make provisions for) : something (as a property or perquisite) claimed as rightful to some position or rank; a grant of said by sovereign or governing apparatus

apostrophe (*uh*-**pos**-tr*uh*-fee; from Greek *apostrophos*, from *apostrephein*, to turn away) : a rhetorical digression, especially as an address directed towards an imaginary or absent person or thing

argumentum ad analogos (ahr-gy*uh*-**men**-t*uh*m ad *uh*-**nal**-*uh*-g*uh*s; Latin, from Greek *analogos*, proportionate) : a fallacy in which an accepted rule for one situation or thing is assumed to be applicable analogically to a situation or thing described as similar; also *argumentum a simili*

ars poetica (ahrz poh-**et**-i-k*uh*; Latin, *ars*, art, *poetica*, poetry) : literary composition, or a treatise concerning such composition

"**ass between two burthens**" (Genesis 49:14) *"Issachar is a strong ass couching down between two burthens: and he saw that settled life was good, and the land was pleasant; and bowed his shoulder to bear, and became a servant unto tribute."*

ataraxia (at-*uh*-**rak**-see-*uh*; Greek, serenity, from *ataraktos* undisturbed) : a state of unperturbable tranquility, and freedom from emotional disturbance

ataxia (*uh*-**tak**-see-*uh*; Greek, *ataxiā*, disorder) : lack of muscular coordination

augur (**aw**-ger; Latin, a diviner, derivative of *augēre*, to augment) 1. to predict, especially from signs or omens 2. one who predicts the future, especially by the flight of birds

badinage (**bad**-n-ij; French, from *badiner*, to jest) : playful or frivolous banter

"**better a ripe pulpit than a fruit tree**" (Herman Melville, *The Confidence Man*, Chap XIII) *"It was sitting under a ripe pulpit, and better such a seat than under a ripe peach-tree"*

brume (broom; Latin *brūma*, contracted from *brevissima diēs* the shortest day) : fog or mist

bulwark (**buhl**-werk; Middle Dutch *bolwerc*, from *bolle*, tree trunk + *werc*, work) 1. a structure raised as a defensive fortification; a rampart 2. something serving as a bulwark; a defense or safeguard

Calvary (**kal**-*vuh*-ree; from the Christian Bible) 1. the hill outside Jerusalem on which Jesus was crucified. Also **Golgotha** 2. any great suffering

casuist (**kazh**-oo-ist; from Latin *cāsus*, fall, chance) : an overly subtle or specious reasoner; a sophist

causatum (**kawz**-at-*uh*m; Latin, effect) : something that is caused; an effect

catastrophe (k*uh*-**tas**-tr*uh*-fee; Greek *katastrephein* to overturn, from *kata-* + *strephein* to turn) : a shift in condition or circumstance leading to violent over throw or ruin

cenotaph (**sen**-*uh*-taf; Greek from kenotaphion; *kenos*, empty + *taphos*, tomb) : a monument erected to those who have died but whose remains lie elsewhere

cerement (**ser**-*uh*-m*uh*nt; French *cirement*) : a burial garment, as a shroud

chaparral (shap-*uh*-**ral**; Spanish, from *chaparra*, evergreen oak) : a dense thicket

cicatrix (**sik**-*uh*-triks; Latin, scar) : a scar made by the formation of new tissue over a healing wound

circumbendibus (sur-k*uh*m-**ben**-d*uh*-b*uh*s; coined from Latin *circum* round about + English *bend* + Latin *-ibus*, ablative ending) : an indirect or circuitous course especially in writing or speaking; circumlocution

civitas dei (**siv**-i-tas **de**-ee; Latin, from *Dē cīvitāte Deī contrā pāgānōs*, On *The City of God against the Pagans*, by Augustine of Hippo) : city of god, in Augustine, as distinguished from 'the earthly city'

cogito (**koh**-gi-toh; Latin, 'I think') : the assemblage of intellectual processes that constitute the ego

colloquy (**kol**-*uh*-kwee; Latin *colloquium*, conversation) : a formal conversation or dialogue

concordat (kon-**kawr**-dat; Latin *concordāre*, to agree) : formal agreement; covenant

conation (koh-**ney**-sh*uh*n; Latin, *conatio*, act of attempting) : psychological processes that lead toward activity, as desire, volition, inclination, etc; an instance of such inclination

connate (**kon**-eyt; Latin *connātus*, to be born with) 1. inborn or inherent 2. akin, congenial 3. originating at the same time

consecution (kon-si-**kyoo**-sh*uh*n; Latin *cōnsecūtiō*, orderly sequence) 1. sequence or succession 2. relation of consequent to antecedent; deduction

contumely (k*uh*n-**too**-m*uh*-lee; Latin *contumēlia*, insolent) : contempt or harsh language arising from arrogance

cortex (**kawr**-teks; Latin, bark) 1. an outer layer of an organ or bodily structure 2. bark, skin, or rind

crepuscule (**krep**-*uh*-skyool; Latin *crepusculum*) : twilight

daub (dawb; Latin *dēalbāre*, to whitewash) 1. to cover or smear with a soft adhesive substance 2. to apply paint with hasty or crude strokes

decreta (dih-**kree**-t*uh*; pl. of decretum, Latin, *principle, decision*) : decrees, ordinances

delictum (dih-**likt**-uhm; Latin, fault) : an offense, a crime

demesne (dih-**meyn**; Anglo-French, from *demeine*) 1. legal possession of land as one's own 2. manorial land possessed by the lord, not held by tenants 3. domain, territory

diathesis (dahy-**ath**-*uh*-sis**;** Greek, from *diatithenai*, disposition, condition) 1. a constitutional predisposition toward a particular state or condition 2. a grammatical feature that describes the relationship between the *verb* and the *subject* (also known as the *agent*) in a sentence (also *voice*)

disport (dih-**spohrt**; from Latin *portāre*, to carry) 1. a playful diversion 2. to amuse 3. to display

dudgeon (**duhj**-*uh*n; unknown origin) : a feeling of offense, indignation, or anger

edulcorate (ih-**duhl**-k*uh*-reyt; Latin, from *dulcis*, sweet) : to free from harshness; make pleasant

El Dorado (el d*uh*-**rah**-doh; Spanish, the gilded one) : a legendary city or historical region of the New World, often thought to be in South America, that was fabled for its great wealth of gold and precious jewels

Elbe (**el**-b*uh*; German placename) : river 720 miles (1159 kilometers) long in the northern part of the Czech Republic and northeastern Germany flowing northwest into the North Sea

emprise (**em**-prahyz; Latin *prehendere*, *prēndere*, to take, grasp) : a chivalrous or adventurous undertaking

encomium (en-**koh**-mee-*uh*m; Greek *enkōmion*, (speech) praising a victor) : warm glowing speech; a formal expression of praise

entr'acte (**an**-trakt; French, from *entre* between + *acte* act) : an interval between two acts of a play or opera

eschaton (**eska**-ton; Greek *eskhatos*, last) : the final event in the divine plan; the end of the world

excursus (ek-**skur**-s*uh*s; Latin, from *excurrere*, to run out) : an incidental digression from the main topic or narrtive line

expiate (**ek**-spee-eyt; Latin, *expiāre*, to atone) : to make amends or atone for

faineance (**fey**-nee-*uh*ns; Old French, *feignant*, idler) : laziness; the state of being idle

farrago (f*uh*-**rah**-goh; Latin *farrāgō*, mixed fodder, hodgepodge, from *far*, *farr*-, a kind of grain) : an assortment or a medley; a hodgepodge

feint (feynt; French, *feindre* 'feign') : a deceptive or pretended blow, thrust, or other movement

fold (fohld; Old English *fald*) 1. any group or community sharing a way of life or holding the same values 2. a small enclosure or pen for sheep or other livestock, where they can be gathered

fungible (**fuhn**-j*uh*-b*uh*l; Latin *fungibilis*) 1. interchangeable; being something (as money or a commodity) of such a nature that one part or quantity may be replaced by another equal part 2. readily adaptable to new situations

grief's drudge (from Herman Melville, *The Confidence Man*, Chapter VI) : *"Of long faces there are two sorts—that of grief's drudge and that of the imposter"*

groat (groht; Old English *grotan*) : a grain exclusive of the hull

guerdon (**gur**-dn; Old French) : recompense, reward

haruspex (**har**-*uh*-speks; Latin) : a diviner in ancient Rome whose predictions are based on inspection of the entrails of sacrificial animals

heresiarch (h*uh*-**ree**-zee-ahrk; Greek *hairesis*, sect) : the originator or chief proponent of a heresy or heretical movement

homunculus (h*uh*-**muhng**-ky*uh*-l*uh*s; Latin, diminutive of *homō*, man) 1. a small human 2. a miniature, fully formed individual thought by the proponents of the biological theory of preformation to be present in the sperm cell

hydrosere (**hahy**-dr*uh*-seer; Greek, *hýdōr*, water + Latin, *serere*, to join) : a sequence of ecological communities originating in an aquatic habitat

hypostasis (hahy-**pos**-t*uh*-sis; Greek *hupostasis*, a standing) 1. substance, essence, or underlying reality; something that has been hypostatized 2. settling of solid particles in a fluid

idem (**id**-em; Latin, same) : something that has been mentioned previously; the same

ignis fatuus (**ig**-nis **fach**-oo-*uh*s; Latin, foolish fire) 1. a phosphorescent light that hovers or flits over swampy ground at night 2. an illusion; a deceptive hope or goal

illation (ih-**ley**-sh*uh*n; Latin *illātiō*, act of bringing in) 1. the act of inferring or drawing conclusions 2. a conclusion drawn; a deduction

immure (i-´myur̈; Latin *immūrāre*) 1. to imprison, to enclose in walls 2. to build into a wall 3. to entomb

importunity (im-pawr-**too**-ni-tee; Latin *importunatus*, to make oneself troublesome) : the quality or state of being urgently demanding; such a demand

inanition (in-*uh*-**nish**-*uh*n; Latin, *inānīre*, to make empty) 1. the exhausted condition that results from lack of nourishment 2. the absence or loss of social, moral, or intellectual vitality 3. the quality or state of being empty

indite (in-**dahyt**; Latin *dictāre*, to compose) 1. write; compose 2. set down in writing

ineluctable (in-i-**luhk**-t*uh*-b*uh*l; Latin *inēluctābilis*, impenetrable) : not to be avoided or escaped; inevitable

intermezzo (in-ter-**met**-soh; Italian, from Latin *intermedius*, intermediate) 1. a brief entertainment between two longer segments or acts 2. a short passage separating the major sections of a lengthy composition or work

Jubilee (**joo**-b*uh*-lee; Hebrew, *yôbēl*, ram, ram's horn) 1. in the Hebrew scriptures, a year of rest observed by the Israelites, during which slaves were set free, alienated property was restored to the former owners, and all the lands were left   untilled 2. a season of celebration

lemma (**lem**-*uh*; Greek, *lambanein*, to take) 1. an auxiliary proposition used in the demonstration of another proposition 2. the argument or theme of a composition prefixed as a title or introduction 3. a glossed word or phrase

lineament (**lin**-ee-*uh*-m*uh*nt; Latin, *līnea*, line) : a distinctive feature or characteristic, especially of the face

lucubration (loo-ky*oo*-**brey**-sh*uh*n; Latin *lucubratio*, study by night) : laborious study; the product of such

malingerer (m*uh*-**ling**-ger-er; French *malingre*, sickly) : one who feigns illness or other incapacity in order to avoid work

marginalia (mahr-j*uh*-**ney**-lee-*uh*; Latin *marginālis*, marginal) : notes in the margins of a book

marl (mahrl; Latin *marga*) : a loose or crumbling earthy deposit

mathesis (ma-**thee**-sis; Greek, acquisition of knowledge) : knowledge, learning

moira (**moi**-r*uh*; Greek, *meros*, share, lot) : personal destiny

mulct (muhlkt; Latin, *mulcta*, fine) : a penalty such as a fine

mulligan stew (**muhl**-i-g*uh*n stoo; unknown origin) : a stew made of bits of various meats and vegetables

ne plus ultra (**nee** pluh **uhl**-tr*uh*; Latin, no more beyond) 1. the highest point, as of excellence or achievement 2. the most profound degree

nihilo (**nee**-*uh*-loh; Latin, as in *ex nihilo*, from out of nothing) : nothing (n.)

noesis/noetic (noh-**ee**-sis/noh-**et**-ik; Greek, understanding, from *noein*, to perceive) 1. the functioning of the intellect; understanding occurring through direct knowledge, i.e., solely through the intellect 2. in Husserl, the subjective aspect of or the act in an intentional experience; distinguished from *noema* 3. in Plato, the highest knowledge, of the eternal forms or ideas contrasted with *dianoia*

nous (noos; Greek, mind) 1. an intelligent purposive principle of the world; in Stoicism, the Logos 2. the rational part of the individual human soul; reason and knowledge as opposed to sense perception 3. in Neoplatonism, the first emanation of the divine, equal to divine reason and containing the cosmos of intelligible beings

numen (**noo**-min; Latin, nod of the head, divine power) 1. divinity presiding over a place; spirit believed by animists to inhabit certain natural phenomena or objects 2. creative energy; genius

obliquity (*uh*-**blik**-wi-tee; Latin, *oblīquus*) 1. indirectness of speech, thought, or movement 2. deviation from proper conduct or thought 3. the quality or condition of being oblique

oculus (**ok**-y*uh*-l*uh*s; Latin, eye) 1. a circular or oval window or opening 2. the organ of sight

ontic (**on**-tik; Greek, *onto*, being) : relating to or having real being

opprobrium (*uh*-**proh**-bree-*uh*m; Latin, *opprobrāre*, to reproach) 1. something that brings disgrace 2. contempt, reproach

osculation (os-ky*uh*-**ley**-sh*uh*n; Latin, *osculum*, kiss) 1. the act of kissing; a kiss 2. a contact, as between two curves or surfaces, at three or more common points

palaver (p*uh*-**lav**-er; Portuguese, *palavra*, speech) 1. idle chatter 2. talk intended to charm or beguile 3. a negotiation or discussion concerning matters in dispute

papule (**pap**-yool; Latin) : a small solid usually round elevation of the skin

paresis (p*uh*-**ree**-sis; Greek, *parienai*, to let fall) : slight or partial paralysis

Parnassian (pahr-**nas**-ee-*uh*n; Greek place name) 1. of or relating to poetry 2. of or relating to a school of French poets of the second half of the 19th century emphasizing metrical form rather than emotion 3. of or relating to the sacred mountain of Parnassus

pars pro toto (pahrz proh **toh**-toh; Latin) : a part (taken) for the whole

pellicle (**pel**-i-k*uh*l; Latin, diminutive of *pellis*, skin) 1. a thin skin or film such as an outer membrane or liquid film 2. a film that reflects a part of the light falling upon it and transmits the rest

peristalsis (per-*uh*-**stawl**-sis; Greek, *peristellein*, to wrap around) : successive waves of involuntary contraction passing along the walls of a hollow muscular structure (such as the esophagus or intestine) and forcing the contents onward

persiflage (**pur**-s*uh*-flahzh; French, *persifler*, to banter) 1. frivolous banter 2. frivolity or mockery in discussing a subject

phenotype (**fee**-n*uh*-tahyp; Greek *phaino*, shining + *tupos*, impression) : the observable characteristics of an organism based on the interaction of its connate form with the environment

phronesis (froh-**nee**-sis; Greek) : in Aristotle, the practical wisdom that allows for the social and political pursuit of ethical imperatives; both necessary to and sufficient for being virtuous

"plucking the dead hairs of a horse's tail with one's teeth..." (from Laurence Stern, *Tristram Shandy*, Chap VII) *"Did not Dr. Kunastrokius, that great man, at his leisure hours, take the greatest delight imaginable in combing of asses tails, and plucking the dead hairs out with his teeth, though he had tweezers always in his pocket?"*

potestas clavium (poh-**tes**-tahs **kley**-vee-*uh*m; Latin, the power of the keys; see Lev Shestov in the work of this title, Part I, aphorism 4) *Catholicism, I repeat, only raised the question whether the philosophers had legally taken possession of the potestas clavium. But the idea of the limitless power that man possesses over heaven and earth came from Socrates' head. And this idea still lives today; it lives in each of us, no matter what our philosophical convictions may be. Each of us imagines that he has in his possession that great truth which opens for him the way leading to the final mystery and to eternal blessedness."*

practicum (**prak**-ti-k*uh*m; Latin, *prācticus*, practical) : a course of study designed to put a previously studied theory into practice

praxis (**prak**-sis; Greek, from *prāssein*, to do) 1. exercise or practice of an art, science, or skill 2. customary practice or conduct

preterit (**pret**-er-it; Latin, *praeteritum*, past tense) 1. bygone, former 2. of, relating to, or being the verb tense that describes a past action or state

prolepsis (proh-**lep**-sis; Greek, *prolambanein*, to anticipate) : the representation or assumption of a future act or development as if presently existing or accomplished

protean (**proh**-tee-*uh*n; Greek, *Proteus*, a sea god who could change shapes at will) 1. readily taking on varied shapes, forms, or meanings 2. displaying considerable variety or diversity

pulmotor (**puhl**-moh-ter; trademark) : an apparatus for pumping oxygen into the lungs during artificial respiration

purl (purl; unknown orig) 1. to edge or finish with lace or embroidery 2. to flow or ripple with a murmuring sound

put in (Nautical Term) : to bring a vessel into port, esp for a brief stay: *we put in for fresh provisions*

raiment (**rey**-m*uh*nt; Old French areement, *array*) : clothing; garments

recto (**rek**-toh; Latin, *rēctus*, straight, right) 1. the side of a leaf (as of a manuscript) that is to be read first 2. a right-hand page

recusant (ri-**kyoo**-z*uh*nt; Latin, *recusare*, to reject) 1. one who refuses to accept or obey established authority; a dissenter 2. a 16th century English Roman Catholic who refused to attend services of the Church of England, a statutory offense

remise (ri-**mahyz**; Latin *remittere*, to send back) 1. to give, grant, or release a claim to; surrender 2. a second thrust made on the same lunge after the first has missed

revenant (**rev**-*uh*-n*uh*nt; French *revenir*, to return) : one who returns after death or long absence

rostrum (**ros**-tru*h*m; Latin *beak*) 1. a dais, pulpit, or other elevated platform for public speaking 2. the curved, beaklike prow of an ancient Roman ship, especially a war galley

saturnalia (sat-er-**ney**-lee-*uh*; Latin, from the pagan festival of Saturn, the Roman god of agriculture) 1. a celebration characterized by unrestrained revelry and often licentiousness 2. excess, abundance

scree (skree; Old Norse *skridha*, landslide) : an accumulation of loose stones or rocky debris lying on a slope or at the base of a hill or cliff

seity (**see**-i-tee; Latin *se*, oneself) : selfhood, personal identity, or something particular to oneself

semblant (**sem**-bl*uh*nt; Old French, *sembler*, to resemble) 1. resembling, like 2. seeming, apparent 3. semblance

semblable (**sem**-bl*uh*-bu*h*l; Old French, *sembler*, to resemble) 1. one that resembles or has much in common with another 2. a resemblance 3. having a resemblance; resembling or like

shibboleth (**shib**-*uh*-lith; Hebrew, from the use of this word in Judges 12:6 as a test to distinguish Gileadites from Ephraimites, the latter pronouncing the word as 'sibboleth', resulting in the slaughter of 42,000 Ephramaites) 1. a word or pronunciation that distinguishes people of one group or class from those of another 2. a custom or practice that betrays one as an outsider

shiver (**shiv**-er; Old High German *scivaro*; splinter) : to break into many small pieces

sinecure (**sahy**-ni-ky*oo*r; Latin *sine cura*, without care) 1. an office or position that requires little or no work and that usually provides an income 2. an ecclesiastical benefice without cure of souls, i.e., without spiritual care or instruction of church members

sirocco (sh*uh*-**rok**-oh; alteration of Arabic *shalūq*) : a hot dust-laden wind from the Libyan deserts that blows on the northern Mediterranean coast

spoliation (spoh-lee-**ey**-sh*uh*n; Latin *spoliātiō*, to despoil) 1. the act of despoiling or plundering 2. the act of injuring especially beyond reclaim

subjunctive (s*uh*b-**juhngk**-tiv; Latin, *subiungere*, to subjoin, subordinate) 1. of, relating to, or being a mood of a verb used in some languages for contingent or hypothetical action 2. a subjunctive construction

succedaneum (suhk-si-**dey**-nee-*uh*m; Latin, *succēdere*, to succeed) : a substitute

summa summarum (**soom**-*uh* suh-**mah**-*ruh*m; Latin) : all in all, on the whole

suppuration (suhp-y*uh*-**rey**-shu*h* n; Latin, *suppurare*) : the formation or discharge of pus

sward (swawrd; Old English *sweard*, skin) 1. a portion of ground covered with grass 2. the grassy surface of land

tares, harvest of (Matthew 13:24) *"The kingdom of heaven is likened unto a man which sowed good seed in his field: But while men slept, his enemy came and sowed tares among the wheat, and went his way. But when the blade was sprung up, and brought forth fruit, then appeared the tares also."*

tegument (**teg**-y*uh*-mu*h* nt; Latin, *tegere*, to cover) : a natural outer covering

terminus ad quem (**tur**-m*uh*-nu*h*s ad **kwem**; Latin, limit to which) : a goal, object, or course of action

213

transect (**tran**-sekt; Latin *trans-* + *secāre*, to cut) : a sample area or strip (as of land)

transhumance, transhumant (trans-**hyoo**-m*uh*ns; Latin *trans-* + *humus*, earth) : the seasonal migration of livestock to suitable grazing grounds

venery (**ven**-*uh*-ree; Latin *vēnārī*, to hunt; Latin *veneria*, desire) 1. the act or sport of hunting; the chase 2. the pursuit of or indulgence in sexual pleasure

volte-face (volt-**fahs**; Italian *voltafaccia*) : a reversal in policy; about-face

voluptuary (v*uh*-**luhp**-choo-er-ee; Latin *voluptārius*, devoted to pleasure) 1. a person devoted or addicted to luxury and sensual pleasures 2. of, relating to, characterized by, or furthering sensual gratification or luxury

weal (weel; Old English *wela*, well) 1. prosperity; happiness 2. the welfare of the community; the general good 3. a ridge on the flesh raised by a blow; a welt